ELEMENTARY A2

ESCAPE FROM PIZZA PALACE

by James Styring and Alastair Lane

RICHMOND MAZES

Richmond Mazes are fun, interactive readers set in a variety of interesting contexts. As you read you have to make decisions and choose how the story develops. These are enjoyable and effective ways to learn and practise English wherever you are.

What they include:

- ■ Engaging, fun stories to keep readers entertained for hours
- ■ Graded language to suit students at all levels
- ■ An interactive approach which puts the reader in control of how the stories develop
- ■ A range of lively characters and surprising storylines
- ■ A rich mixture of audio and colour illustrations which brings the stories to life
- ■ A glossary section to check the meaning of all business vocabulary
- ■ Lots of opportunity to re-read the story making different decisions and finding new routes through the maze.

See if you can find your way through the maze!

Introduction

This story and other Richmond Mazes can also
be downloaded onto Apple and Android devices.
Available from the iTunes App Store and Google Play.

Escape from Pizza Palace

In this maze, the goal is to find the job of your dreams, but to do this you must make the correct decisions.

 Read the story carefully, look at the different options and then turn to the correct section to make your decision.

 You can win bonus points as you move through the story. If you win a bonus point, mark it on the scorecard on page 115.

 If you make a bad decision, you will have to start the chapter again.

 Sometimes you have to write down important information. If you see this symbol, write down the information on page 115.

 You can listen to the audio at **https://mod.lk/pizza**

degree* You can check the meaning of words with this symbol in the glossary on page 116.

Good luck!

Chapter 1

Section 1

You graduated from university three months ago. You've got a good degree* but no work and no money, so you're living with your parents. You're looking for your first job. For the moment you're happy to work in a supermarket or a café, but really you want to find a good job. You want a professional career*.

One day you see a job advert* in a pizza restaurant. You go inside and ask to speak to the manager. The manager's got a pink face and a friendly smile. She looks into your eyes while she's shaking your hand. 'I'm Ruth Friers. I'm the manager here. We're looking for kitchen staff*. You don't need any experience. There's a part-time* job – mainly evening shifts*, and there's a full-time* job too. Are you interested?'

Chapter 1

> **Do you ...**
> 1 accept the part-time position? It's not a great job, but you can earn some money and you'll have time for your job search. ▶ section 2
> 2 accept the full-time position? This is your first job and you need lots of work experience. ▶ section 7

2 Section 2

After three days at Pizza Palace, you're very tired. 'Don't worry,' says Ruth. 'Everyone is tired in their first week. It's a new job and you have to learn a lot. Soon, you'll find the job quite easy!'

As a student, you loved Pizza Palace. Their pizzas are big and cheap. As a member of staff, you don't love Pizza Palace. They pay you the minimum wage* and the work is boring. But the job is easy, so you work hard and the manager likes you.

One day, Ruth asks, 'Can we change your shift? You can either work a full-time shift 14.30–22.30, or you can work flexible shifts.'

'What are flexible shifts?' you ask.

'With a flexible shift, you work lots of different hours – sometimes in the mornings, or maybe late at night. It depends on what I need. We can pay you a little more.'

> **Do you ...**
> 1 choose the full-time shift? In the mornings, you can find a better job. ▶ section 9
> 2 choose flexible shifts? You want longer hours and more pay. ▶ section 4

3 Section 3

You phone your friend Mark and ask him to help you with your job search. The only problem is time.

'I'm really busy this week,' he says. 'I'm only free* in the evenings, when you're working at Pizza Palace.'

6

Chapter 1

'OK,' you tell Mark. 'Maybe next week.'

▶ section 12

Section 4

Flexible shifts weren't a good choice. Ruth usually gives you 11.30–13.30, 17.30–19.30 and 22.30–00.30. That's only six hours, and there isn't time to go home between shifts.

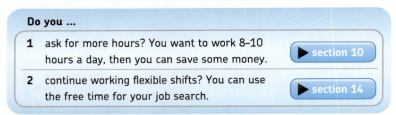

Section 5

You register on the recruitment agent's website and pay the fee. You wait for an email or a phone call, but you don't hear anything. After five weeks, you call the recruitment agent's number. An electronic voice says, 'This number does not exist. Please try again.'

Bad luck! Your job search ends here.

Go back to the start of the chapter and try again. ◀ section 1

Section 6

Good choice! Ruth thinks you can do the job and it's only for a few days. This experience will be great for your CV*.

▶ section 16

Section 7

After three days at Pizza Palace, you're very tired. 'It's OK,' says Ruth. 'New staff are always tired because there's a lot to learn. Soon, you'll find the job quite easy!'

One day, Ruth has a meeting with the staff in the restaurant. 'I'm

Chapter 1

sorry everyone. There isn't enough work at the moment. I need to change your shifts. You have two options. You can work flexible shifts or late-night shifts.'

'What are flexible shifts?' someone asks.

'With a flexible shift, you always work different hours. Sometimes you work mornings and lunchtimes, or maybe you work at night. It depends on what I need. We'll pay you a little more.'

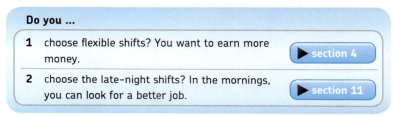

Do you ...

1. choose flexible shifts? You want to earn more money. ▶ section 4
2. choose the late-night shifts? In the mornings, you can look for a better job. ▶ section 11

8 Section 8

One morning, you meet your friend Simon. He's also looking for a job. He tells you about a recruitment agent*. The agent has got contacts at hundreds of big companies. The agent says he can find anyone a good job in six weeks. You can register* on his website, but you have to pay a fee.* It's very expensive – one month's pay!

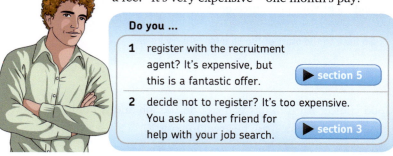

Do you ...

1. register with the recruitment agent? It's expensive, but this is a fantastic offer. ▶ section 5
2. decide not to register? It's too expensive. You ask another friend for help with your job search. ▶ section 3

9 Section 9

You're working full-time now and you're very busy. You're earning more money, but you haven't got time for your job search. You're getting worried. You don't want to stay at Pizza Palace for too long.

Chapter 1

Section 10

Ruth gives you a long shift – 07.00–17.00. After a few weeks, you're very, very tired again. You forget orders*, you drop food and one day, you burn twelve pizzas.

In the end, Ruth says, 'I'm very sorry, but you're making too many mistakes. I need to ask you to leave.'

Bad luck! Your job search ends here.

Go back to the start of the chapter and try again.

Section 11

You're working late-night shifts now. You get home very late every night, sometimes at 03.00 a.m. You're too tired to look for jobs in the mornings. You're getting worried. You don't want to stay at Pizza Palace for too long.

Section 12

You continue working hard at Pizza Palace. Some days you work in the kitchens with the chef, and other days you serve customers at the tables. You often help Ruth when she's too busy. You're learning

Chapter 1

a lot about working as part of a team and you're getting good work experience.

▶ section 13

13 Section 13

The next morning your mobile phone rings at 8.30 a.m. You're very tired, but you get out of bed and look for the phone. You find it, but it's too late – the phone stops ringing. One minute later, the phone beeps. You have a new voicemail.

'Hello, I'm calling from Pizza Palace Human Resources* department. It's about Ruth Friers, your manager. Unfortunately, she's ill and she can't come to work for a few days. We need someone to do her job. Ms Friers suggested you. If you're interested, please call me.'

Do you ...
1. call the HR department? Maybe this is a great opportunity.   ▶ section 6
2. decide not to call? You're very tired and Ruth's job is too difficult.   ▶ section 15

14 Section 14

⭐ You win 1 bonus point. Mark the scorecard on page 115.
The café next door has free WiFi. When you have a break at work, you go to the café with your laptop and you look for jobs online.

▶ section 12

15 Section 15

Good choice! Sometimes it's important to say 'no' to offers.

▶ section 16

10

Chapter 2

Section 16

To find a good job you need to write a new CV*. You ask your friend Mark to help you. Mark finished university last year. Now he works as a journalist* for a local newspaper, the *Newtown Times*. You meet in a café. Mark's wearing a designer jumper and some very cool* sunglasses. You ask for a coffee and you sit down together. You show Mark your old CV. 'How do I write a good CV?' you ask.

Mark looks at your old CV. He puts his fingers together and thinks. 'Don't put the words 'CV' on it. Just write your name at the top.'

'OK,' you say.

'You also have a silly email address, crazywolf@email.com. It's not very professional. Change it to something like mine, marksmith@email.com.'

'Good idea,' you reply.

'Wait a minute,' says Mark and he opens his bag. He takes out a piece of paper and gives it to you. It's his CV. 'Don't write a new CV,' he says. 'Just copy my one. Change the name and the personal information. I got a great job with my CV.'

Mark's uncle is the editor* of the *Newtown Times*. You think this is how Mark got his job, but you don't say this.

11

Chapter 2

'Thanks, Mark,' you say. You finish your coffee and then you go home to write your new CV.

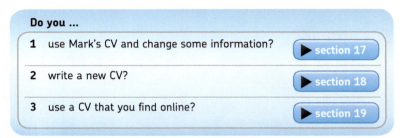

Section 17

When you get home, you look at Mark's CV. He's got a lot of personal information on his CV.

You decide to call Mark.

Section 18

You need to include work experience on your CV, but your only work experience is your job at Pizza Palace. You don't think your CV looks very interesting. On the other hand, you know that lots of people don't write the truth on their CVs. Some people lie* about their work. You could invent jobs so the work experience section looks more interesting.

Chapter 2

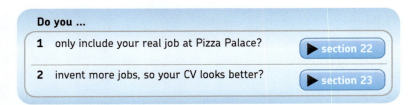

Section 19

This CV has a virus! When you email the CV to companies, the virus sends thousands and thousands of emails to other people. You can't stop it!

You only receive one reply* to your CV.

Bad decision! Now you need a different CV.

Section 20

'I still don't think it's a good idea to include all those hobbies*,' says Mark, 'but it's your decision.'

'I'm not a robot,' you say. 'Hobbies are important.'

'OK, OK. Now look at my CV again. Do you see the photo? I think it's a good idea to put a photo on a CV. It helps people to see you as a person. A professional photographer took my photo.'

You look at Mark's photo on his CV. The photo doesn't really look like him.

Chapter 2

21 Section 21

'All right,' says Mark. 'I'm just trying to help you! I'm sure your CV is fine.'

Mark looks a bit angry but he doesn't say anything more.

22 Section 22

You finish your CV. The next day you show it to Mark.
He reads it. 'What's this on your CV?' he asks. 'Professor Thorpe? Clara Wilson?'

'They're my references*,' you say. 'Professor Thorpe knew me as a student and Clara Wilson is a family friend. Every CV has references.'

'No, they don't! People don't want to see references on a CV. Don't include them on your CV.'

You think about Mark's idea. Maybe he's right, but Professor Thorpe is very famous.

23 Section 23

At one company, the managing director reads your CV and thinks it's great. Unfortunately, she then gives your CV to her assistant. The assistant spends an hour on Google and Facebook to check the CV.

Chapter 2

They have a meeting later that day. 'What do you think?' asks the managing director. 'This CV is perfect!'

'Yeah,' says the assistant. 'Too perfect. This CV is full of lies. Nothing in it is true.'

'I see,' says the managing director. 'In that case, don't invite this person for an interview*. Let's look at the other CVs.'

Unfortunately, other companies also check your CV. Your lies are too obvious and everyone sees them. Your CV looks great, but nobody believes* it.

Bad luck! Your job search ends here.

Go back to the start of the chapter and try again. section 16

Section 24

'No photo? Personally, I think it's a mistake,' says Mark. 'A CV needs a photo.'

'Well, I'm happy to a have a CV without a photo,' you say.

'It's your decision,' he says. 'OK, it's time for my horse riding class. I have to go. Speak to you later!'

'Thanks for your help. Bye!' you say.

Now it's time to send the CV to employers.

 section 29

Section 25

'OK, OK, it's your decision,' says Mark. 'But look, your CV is three pages. That's too long. You need a two-page CV. You must cut something.'

What do you say?

1	'Thanks for your advice, Mark, but I'm happy with my CV.'	▶ section 21
2	'Two pages is better, but how can I write a two-page CV and keep the references?'	▶ section 27

Chapter 2

26 Section 26

⭐ You win 1 bonus point. Mark the scorecard on page 115.
Good decision! Your CV doesn't need to include all your hobbies. You only need the ones that are interesting to an employer*, like your dance class. That shows you are good at working with other people. The phone call continues. 'Your CV is very well-organised, Mark,' you say.

'Yes, I think it's an excellent CV,' he says.

Mark's CV includes information about his education and his work experience. The most recent information appears first.

Education
2010–2013   Central University
             BA in Journalism
2006–2010   City High School

Work Experience
2012–Current Journalist, The *Newtown Times*
2011–2012   Assistant Manager, Astra Cinema

Mark also has a photo on his CV.

Do you ...
1 decide not to include a photo? ▶ section 24
2 include a photo with your CV?   ▶ section 29

27 Section 27

'OK, you want to keep the references, but you also want a two-page CV,' says Mark. 'Well, maybe use a smaller font*. With smaller writing, all the information will fit on two pages.'

To change the font, you change this:

2012–Current   Working at Pizza Palace

Chapter 2

To this:

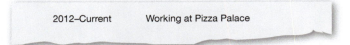

'There's also a photo,' you say. 'I can cut the photo and keep the references.'

Do you ...

1 use a smaller font on your CV? ▶ section 29

2 cut the photo? ▶ section 24

Section 28

'How are you getting on?' asks Mark. 'I'm sure it'll be easy with my CV.'

Mark always thinks he's an expert* on everything. 'Er, yes,' you say. 'It's interesting. You included your hobbies on the CV.'

'That's right,' says Mark.

'I have lots of hobbies too,' you say. 'Yoga, tennis, rollerblading, and I go to a dance class.'

'Hmm ...' says Mark. 'Don't include all of those hobbies. There are too many for your CV.'

What do you say?

1 'I don't agree. I want to include all of the hobbies.' ▶ section 20

2 'You're right. I'll only include some of the hobbies.' ▶ section 26

Chapter 3

29 Section 29

You are happy with your CV*. Now it's time to look for jobs. You look in newspapers and online. You don't see many good jobs advertised. In the end, you find five job adverts.

Which email do you send with your CV?

1

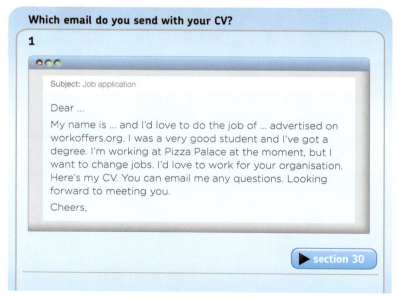

Subject: Job application

Dear …

My name is … and I'd love to do the job of … advertised on workoffers.org. I was a very good student and I've got a degree. I'm working at Pizza Palace at the moment, but I want to change jobs. I'd love to work for your organisation. Here's my CV. You can email me any questions. Looking forward to meeting you.

Cheers,

▶ section 30

Chapter 3

Section 30

You send job applications* to the five companies. After three weeks, there are no replies. Maybe they aren't interested in you, and you need to apply* for more jobs.

'Is it normal for companies not to reply?' you think. 'Is there a problem with my email or with my CV?'

Do you ...	
1 apply for more jobs?	▶ section 36
2 think again about your applications?	▶ section 40

Section 31

You call one of the companies and explain about the mistakes. 'Don't worry about it,' says the receptionist. 'I'm sure it doesn't matter, but if you want, you can send us the CV again.'

You call the other companies and they say the same thing.

▶ section 44

19

Chapter 3

32 Section 32

You look in the newspaper and on the internet again and you find three new job adverts. You send each company an email and your CV. You wait two weeks, but there are no replies.

'Is this bad luck?' you ask yourself. 'Or is there a problem with my applications?'

You look at your CV and think about how you can make it better. Suddenly, you notice two mistakes! You made a spelling mistake and the years for your time at school were wrong.

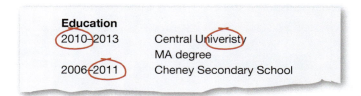

Do you ...

1	call each company to explain your mistakes?	▶ section 31
2	ask somebody for advice?	▶ section 35
3	send the CVs to the companies again?	▶ section 39

33 Section 33

You find an agency online that writes CVs and job applications. You send them two job adverts. The next day they send you a new CV and two job application letters. You read them and they're terrible! Now you've got no money, no time and no job interviews.

Bad luck! Your job search ends here.

Go back to the start of the chapter and try again. ◀ section 29

Chapter 3

Section 34

⭐ You win 1 bonus point. Mark the scorecard on page 115.
Good decision! There are special phrases for job applications. You always need to use these phrases.

▶ section 42

Section 35

You call your friend Amy – she always has good advice*. You tell her about the mistakes in your CV.

'Spelling mistakes *can* be a problem. Always check everything carefully before you press 'send'. Don't worry about it now, though,' Amy says. 'Maybe no one will see your mistakes. Many companies only read a CV for about 10 seconds before they decide 'yes' or 'no'. If you get an interview, you can tell them about the mistakes then.'

'OK,' you say. 'Thanks for the advice!'

▶ section 44

Section 36

You send ten more job applications. You wait a month, and there are still no replies.

You call your friend Amy. She's looking for a job too. Maybe she has some good advice. Amy is great at some things and very bad at others. She's always late, she forgets appointments and she loses things like her phone and her purse. But Amy's clever* and she's good at solving problems.

'There are a lot of good companies in this area,' you say. 'Most of the companies haven't got job adverts on their websites, but maybe I can write to them to ask for work. What do you think?'

'Don't email companies if they aren't advertising jobs,' she says. 'Most companies haven't got time to answer lots of emails from jobseekers*.'

'But I can still write to them, can't I?' you say.

21

Chapter 3

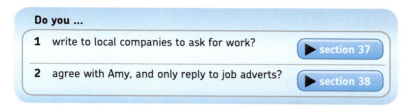

Section 37

You write to thirty local companies. It takes a long time to find their email addresses. After six weeks, there is only one reply.

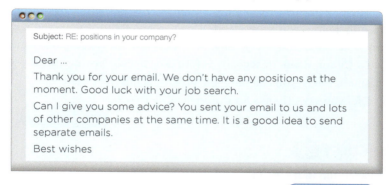

Section 38

You're working hard at Pizza Palace. You haven't got much time to look for jobs, but you're saving money. You decide to spend some money on your job search.

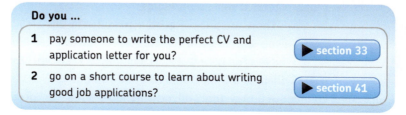

Chapter 3

Section 39

You send an email to the companies with the corrected CV attached. This email asks employers to delete the previous CV and to read the new one.

Section 40

You decide to meet your friend Amy. She's looking for a job too. Maybe she has some good advice. Amy's great at some things and very bad at others. She's always late, she forgets appointments and she loses things like her phone and her purse. But Amy's clever* and she's good at solving problems.

'Have a look at my applications. What can I do?'
Amy reads your emails and the CV.

'The CV's OK,' she says. 'But the email isn't great. There are special phrases for job applications. I did a course. It was brilliant. I'll give you my notes.'

'Thanks,' you say, 'but there aren't any interesting jobs at the moment. Companies aren't advertising positions, but there are a lot of good companies in this area. Maybe I can ask them for work.'

'It's your decision,' says Amy.

Section 41

You learn a lot about how to write a good application.
   Now you've got a good application email with the right phrases.

Chapter 3

> Subject: Job application
>
> Dear ...
> I am writing to apply for the position of ..., as advertised on workoffers. org website. I have an MA from Central University. At the moment, I have a temporary job at Pizza Palace, where I have a lot of experience of working with customers. I believe I have the qualities necessary for the position.
> My CV is attached. Thank you for considering my application. Please contact me if you need further information. I look forward to hearing from you.
> Kind regards,

▶ section 32

42 Section 42

You send your email and CV to the five companies. After three weeks, there is only one reply. The company tells you that the position isn't available anymore.

You decide to call your friend Amy. Amy's looking for a job too. Maybe she can give you some advice. Amy's great at some things and very bad at others. She's always late, she forgets appointments and she loses things like her phone and her purse. But Amy is clever* and she's good at solving problems.

▶ section 43

43 Section 43

You meet Amy. She arrives late as usual, but you don't say anything. You show her your CV and the email you sent to the companies.

'Your CV looks OK,' says Amy. 'I don't see a problem. Show me your email.'

You are a bit worried. Amy looked at your CV very quickly. Maybe she missed a mistake?

Now Amy's reading the email so you don't say anything. Amy looks at you. She reads the email

Chapter 3

again. Then she smiles. 'Oh, dear!' she laughs. 'Did you send the email to all the companies at the same time?'

'Yes, why?'

'That's not a good idea. You should send each company a separate email,' she says.

▶ section 32

Chapter 4

Section 44

The next morning before your shift at Pizza Palace, you meet your friend Simon. He was at school with you. Now he's looking for a job too. He invites you to play tennis with him. It's a hot day and he plays very hard. He really wants to win. In the middle of the game, you hear your phone ringing. 'Don't answer it!' says Simon. 'We're playing a game!'

You want to answer the phone but Simon looks serious. 'OK,' you say.

The game ends and Simon wins. Quickly, you run to your mobile phone. There's a voicemail but you don't recognise the number. You listen carefully to the message. It's about a job interview!

Section 45

'Hello, this is Dr Carol Tree from the City Museum. You sent your CV to us last week. We're looking for someone to work as a PA* in the museum office. We'd like to invite you for an interview this Friday at 2.00 p.m. If you're interested, please call me back on this number – 01632 960 912. Thanks.'

Chapter 4

'What is it?' Simon asks. 'What is it?'

'I have a job interview,' you say. 'On Friday. It's for a PA job in the City Museum.'

'Friday?' says Simon. 'No, you can't go that day. It's Amy's birthday. We're all going for lunch.'

'But it's a job interview!' you say.

'Yes,' says Simon. 'But only for a job as a PA. A PA is a personal assistant. It's a kind of secretary. A PA organises meetings, makes coffee for the boss*, and answers emails and the phone. You don't want that job – it's not good enough for you.'

It's a difficult decision. It's a job interview, but Amy will be disappointed* if you don't celebrate her birthday.

Do you ...

1	decide not to phone Dr Tree because you don't want a PA job?	▶ section 48
2	phone Dr Tree and agree to the interview?	▶ section 51
3	phone Dr Tree and try to change the date of the interview?	▶ section 55

Section 46

Simon told you not to go the interview. Now, he's at the interview for the job and you're at Amy's party.

You want to go home. You leave the restaurant and cross the road. You're thinking about Simon, when suddenly there's a terrible noise and everything goes black.

You wake up in hospital. Your leg is broken. You can't move from your bed for four months.

Bad luck! Your job search ends here.

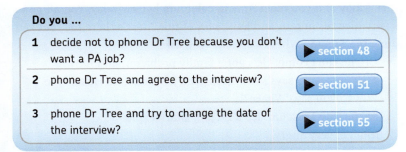

Go back to the start of the chapter and try again. ◀ section 44

Chapter 4

Section 47

'Oh, well, you can look around the museum after the interview,' says Dr Tree. She asks you some questions but the interview finishes in just twenty minutes.

Afterwards, you look around the museum. Before you leave, you see Dr Tree in her office with a young man in a suit*. They are talking and laughing.

You decide to go home and wait for Dr Tree to call.

 section 61

Section 48

It is Friday and you meet Amy to celebrate her birthday. You all go to a very nice restaurant and have a lot of fun. Mark's there too, but you don't see Simon. 'Where's Simon?' you ask.

'Oh, he can't come. He's got a family problem,' says Amy.
'That's not true,' says Mark. 'He's got a job interview. He told me.'
'What?' you say. 'Where?'
'At the City Museum. It's a PA job,' Mark explains.
You feel very angry.

 section 46

Section 49

It's Friday at 2.00 p.m. You have the interview in Dr Tree's office. She's very friendly, but also professional.

'Please come in. Take a seat,' she says. 'So, tell me. Why do you want this job? Why do you want to be a PA in a museum?'

What do you say?

1 'At the moment, I'm working at Pizza Palace and I hate it. I really want a real job with a career.'   section 60

2 'I really want to work in a museum. I think museums are fascinating.'   ▶ section 50

Chapter 4

Section 50

'I'm pleased,' says Dr Tree. 'It's great that you're enthusiastic about the job.'

'Next question. Do you like working in a team or on your own?'

What do you say?

1 'I like working in a team'. ▶ section 54

2 'I like working on my own'. ▶ section 57

Section 51

⭐ You win 1 bonus point. Mark the scorecard on page 115.

You phone Amy. 'Bad news. I can't have lunch on Friday for your birthday,' you say. 'I've got a job interview that day.'

'That's OK,' says Amy. 'A job interview is more important. Good luck!'

Then you call Dr Tree. She's very pleased to speak to you. 'Thank you for calling me back so quickly,' she says. 'The job is in the City Museum. The successful* candidate* will be my PA.'

You agree to go for the interview. Before the interview, you visit the museum. There are rooms with Greek statues, old clothes, and paintings from around the world. It's a very beautiful building. It's a very nice place to work.

▶ section 49

Chapter 4

52 Section 52

'Hi,' you say. 'Are you here for the interview?'

'Yes, I am,' the man says. 'I'm an old friend of Carol's. She told me about the job last week.'

You hear Dr Tree call from inside the office. 'Jimmy! Hi, come in. I'm so pleased to see you.' she says.

'Excuse me,' Jimmy says to you.

'Good luck,' you say, but you don't mean it.

section 61

53 Section 53

The next day, you do the early-morning shift at Pizza Palace. Then you go for your interview at the City Museum.

'Hello,' says Dr Tree. 'Pleased to meet you. What do you think of our museum?'

What do you say?

1. 'I'm sorry, but I didn't have time to look at the museum.' — section 47
2. 'I love the Egyptian art.' — section 58

54 Section 54

'Ah, that might be a problem,' says Dr Tree. 'You have to work on your own in this job because I travel a lot for work.'

'I like working on my own too,' you say.

'Oh, really?' Dr Tree replies. She asks you some more questions before the end of the interview, but you don't think it was a success*. Finally you say goodbye and leave. You see another man waiting outside Carol Tree's office. He's wearing a suit*.

You go home and wait for Dr Tree's call.

section 61

30

Chapter 4

Section 55

Dr Tree answers the phone. You say your name and you explain your problem. 'I'm sorry but I'm not free* on Friday,' you say.

'Oh, I'm sorry to hear that,' says Dr Tree. She says 'sorry' but she doesn't sound happy. 'Let's see,' she says. 'Is next week convenient for you? How about Tuesday afternoon?'

'Yes, that's fine for me,' you say. 'Thank you for changing the day.'

This is good news. You can have lunch with Amy on her birthday, you can visit the museum at the weekend and you can have the interview on Tuesday.

The next morning, your phone rings again.

▶ section 59

Section 56

'OK,' says Dr Tree. 'Come for the interview this afternoon. It's the only other possible time.'

'OK,' you say. You feel bad about this situation.

When you go the museum, Dr Tree is friendly, but she's not very interested in you. She doesn't give you any information about the job. She only asks you about your job at Pizza Palace. After five minutes, her mobile rings. 'Excuse me,' she says. 'Let's end the interview here. Thank you for coming.'

She shakes your hand. She answers her phone before you leave her office.

▶ section 61

31

Chapter 4

57   Section 57

'That's good,' says Dr Tree. 'I often travel for work. So, if you are my PA, you'll work on your own a lot here.'

She seems pleased. She asks you some more questions and you answer them. Finally you say goodbye and you leave. You see another man waiting outside Dr Tree's office. He's wearing a suit*.

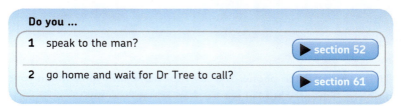

Do you …
1 speak to the man? ▶ section 52
2 go home and wait for Dr Tree to call? ▶ section 61

58   Section 58

Dr Tree's face changes. She doesn't smile. The interview continues but you don't answer her questions very well. She doesn't seem friendly now. At the end, she invites you to look around the museum. You see there's no Egyptian art. Dr Tree knows you lied* to her.

Before you leave, you see Dr Tree in her office with a young man in a suit*. They're talking and laughing.

You don't think that the interview was a success*.

▶ section 61

59   Section 59

'I'm sorry,' says Dr Tree. 'Now it's my turn! I need to change the time of your interview. Can you come for the interview tomorrow?'

Tomorrow! You'll have no time to visit the museum before the interview.

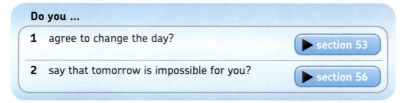

Do you …
1 agree to change the day? ▶ section 53
2 say that tomorrow is impossible for you? ▶ section 56

Chapter 4

Section 60

Dr Tree looks surprised.

You realise that it was a mistake to complain* about your job. She writes something in her notebook. She asks you some more questions but the interview is only twenty minutes long. When it ends, she says goodbye and you leave.

You see another person outside Dr Tree's office. This person is the same age as you. He's wearing a suit*.

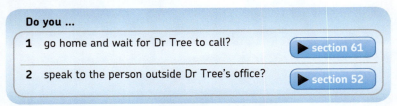

Do you ...

1 go home and wait for Dr Tree to call? ▶ section 61

2 speak to the person outside Dr Tree's office? ▶ section 52

Chapter 5

Section 61

The next day, you're working the evening shift at Pizza Palace. You talk to your colleagues in the restaurant. You tell them about the interview at the museum. 'I know they won't call me. It wasn't a good interview,' you say.

'Why not?' asks Darren, the chef. Darren's very friendly and kind. He always talks to the staff at Pizza Palace when they have a problem.

'I'm sure she didn't like me. The interview was short. She didn't ask many questions. And there was somebody else for the interview – a man in a suit. I think he was friends with the interviewer. I'm sure he'll get the job.'

'Don't worry,' says Darren. 'It was only your first interview.'

'I suppose so. It was a really nice place, though. I wanted to start my career there,' you say.

'Never mind,' he says. 'You applied for other jobs.'

'Yes,' you say, 'I can wait. I'll probably get more interviews. And I need to save some money! Maybe I can get more shifts at Pizza Palace.'

'Look,' says Darren, 'if you want, you can call the interviewer. Ask her about the interview.'

'Can I do that?' you reply.

Chapter 5

Do you ...	
1 work more shifts at Pizza Palace and apply for jobs?	▶ section 63
2 call Dr Tree about the job at the City Museum?	▶ section 67
3 ask some friends for advice?	▶ section 76

Section 62

You read about a careers fair* on LinkedIn. The careers fair is at your old university next week. It's going to be really big. Two hundred employers will have stands* there. You arrange to go.

▶ section 77

Section 63

You forget about the museum. You're busy at Pizza Palace most days. Other days, you have a little time to continue your job search.

One day, when you finish your shift, you look at your mobile phone. You see you have a voicemail message. 'Wow!' you think. 'Maybe it's about a job.'

'Hello, this is Graham Goldsmith. I work for Santmundo Publishing. We're looking for an editorial assistant* at the moment and Carol Tree sent us a copy of your CV – I liked it. Are you still looking for work? If you're interested, please ring me on 01632 960 122 and I'll arrange an interview.'

You phone Graham Goldsmith, but there's no answer, so you leave a message. You say, 'Hello Mr Goldsmith, thank you for your message. I'm still looking for work and I'd love to come for an interview. Please call me when you get this message. Thanks very much and I'm looking forward to speaking with you soon.'

▶ section 66

Chapter 5

Section 64

You Google your name. There are 140,000 results. You look for the photos of you at the party. You search for images. There aren't any photos of you in the first 150 photos. You forget about the problem and continue with your job search.

 section 62

Section 65

You call Santmundo Publishing and ask for Graham Goldsmith. 'Hello,' says a woman. 'Who is this?' You explain the situation.

'I'm very sorry. Graham Goldsmith doesn't work here now.'
Bad luck! Your job search ends here.

Go back to the start of the chapter and try again. section 61

Section 66

You wait a few days, but Graham Goldsmith doesn't contact you. You feel nervous about the interview with Santmundo Publishing.

After two more days, you ring Graham Goldsmith again. Nobody answers, so you leave another message. You say, 'Hello, Mr Goldsmith. You called me a few days ago about a job at Santmundo publishing – an editorial assistant. I just wanted to say that I'm very interested in the position and I'd like to have an interview. Thank you very much.'

You look at your phone a lot, but Graham Goldsmith doesn't call.

Do you ...
1. call Santmundo Publishing and ask to speak to Graham Goldsmith? section 65
2. wait for Graham Goldsmith to contact you? section 68

Section 67

⭐ You win 1 bonus point. Mark the scorecard on page 115.

You call Carol Tree at the City Museum. 'Hi,' she says. 'Didn't you get

Chapter 5

a call?'

'A call?' you say. 'No, I didn't.'

'It's bad news, I'm afraid. You didn't get the job. I asked Jimmy to call you. Maybe he forgot.'

'That's OK,' you say. 'Who's Jimmy?'

'He's my new PA.'

You're a bit annoyed* – this was the man who had an interview after you.

'Can I ask about the interview?'

'Yes.'

'Can I ask why didn't I get the job?'

'Well, it was a hard decision. In the end I chose Jimmy because he had a lot of experience. But you were very good, too.'

'Oh, right. Thank you.'

'I have some good news, I hope. I know an editor at a small publishing company. His name's Graham Goldsmith. They're looking for an editorial assistant*. I can mention you to Graham and send him your CV.'

'Really? That's great! Thank you.'

Well done! It was a good idea to call and ask why you didn't get the job.

▶ section 63

Section 68

Graham Goldsmith never contacts you. You meet your friends Mark and Simon on your free day. You tell them about Santmundo and Graham Goldsmith.

'Don't worry,' says Mark. 'I'm sure you'll find something soon. Have you got a good online profile*?'

'A what?' you ask.

'An online profile,' says Simon. 'You've got Facebook and Twitter, you can use them to look for jobs. And why don't you write a blog? That's a great way to create an online profile.'

'Or register* on LinkedIn,' says Mark. 'Millions of employers use LinkedIn.'

▶ section 71

Chapter 5

Section 69

One day you get a call from Amy. 'There are some really bad photos of you on Facebook,' she says.

'What do you mean?'

'There are some photos of you at crazy parties, when you were at university. Employers won't like them! They won't like your image.'

'But nobody can see my photos, except friends,' you say. 'My Facebook page is private.'

'Yes, but they aren't on *your* Facebook page. They're on Maria's page and her account isn't private. You're tagged in the photos, so anyone could Google your name and see them.'

'Oh, no! Who's Maria?' you ask.

'She's Simon's sister.'

You don't know Maria.

Do you …

1 do nothing? ▶ section 64

2 contact Maria via Facebook? ▶ section 74

3 contact Simon? ▶ section 75

Section 70

You decide to register on LinkedIn. It's really easy to use. You can copy your CV into it, and you can add lots of extra information. You can link with people who have jobs and you can join groups. It's brilliant.

▶ section 69

Section 71

You look at your Facebook and Twitter accounts.

On Facebook, there are lots of silly photos from your days at university, so you delete them. You don't want employers* to see those photos. Then you make your Facebook account private, so in future, only friends can see your posts and photos.

On Twitter, there are some conversations that you don't want employers to read, so you delete your history. You start to follow some interesting companies. You can see that Twitter is going to be useful in your job search.

Now you need an online profile. You haven't got time to start a blog *and* create a LinkedIn profile. You can only choose one.

Section 72

You write your first blog. It takes six hours. You send it to Simon. He doesn't like it. He sends it back with lots of changes. You write it again. This time you don't send it to Simon. You post it online. A week later, you have three hits. The visitors are Simon, Amy and Mark.

After two months, you have eighteen blog entries and nine hits. All of the visitors are friends. Employers can't find you because you don't come high in a Google search.

Section 73

You love LinkedIn. It's really easy to use and it's free. You can copy your CV into it, and you can add lots of extra information. You can link with people who have jobs and you can join groups. LinkedIn is very popular and you notice that a few employers are looking at your profile.

Section 74

You become friends with Simon's sister Maria on Facebook. You message her:

Chapter 5

New message

Me (15:07)
Hi. I'm Simon's friend from school. Remember me?

Maria (15:07)
Hi! Sure!

Me (15:08)
Why did you put those pictures of me on your wall? Where did you get them?

Maria (15:08)
What pictures?

Me (15:09)
There are some photos of me at a party. From when I was at university.

Maria (15:12)
I don't know what you're talking about ... Oh, now I can see the photos, but I didn't post them!

Me (15:12)
What?

Maria (15:13)
Maybe Simon posted them, he used my laptop yesterday. They're really funny! LOL

Me (15:13)
They aren't funny for employers.

Maria (15:14)
What?

Me (15:14)
I'm looking for a job. If an employer looks for my name on the internet, they can see the photos on your page. Can you delete them?

Maria (15:17)
OK ... Deleted!

Me (15:18)
Great. Thanks!

▶ section 62

Chapter 5

Section 75

You call Simon. 'Hi,' you say. 'It's me. Why did you put those pictures of me on Facebook?'

'What pictures?'

'There are some photos of me at a party. From when I was at university.'

'Oh, I forgot! I posted some old photos last night. They're funny!'

'They aren't funny for employers. I'm tagged in the photos. If an employer Googles my name, they can find the photos. Can you delete them?'

'OK, I'm looking at my Facebook page now ... I can't see any photos of you. Where are they?'

'They're on your sister's page.'

'What? Oh, I remember. I had Maria's laptop last night. Maybe I forgot to log off her account and into mine. Maybe I posted them on her wall by mistake.'

'By mistake?' You don't believe him.

'Yes, by mistake. Listen, don't worry. I'll tell her to delete them.'

'OK. Thanks.'

Section 76

You meet Amy. She says, 'Everyone finds work via social media these days.'

'What do you mean?' you ask.

'You know, Facebook and Twitter and things like that,' replies Amy.

'But Facebook and Twitter are personal,' you say. 'How can social media help me find work?'

'You can follow companies. Then you know what they're doing, and you might see a job advert. And don't forget, you need to have an online profile*,' says Amy. 'Why don't you write a blog? And register* on LinkedIn? Millions of employers* use LinkedIn.'

41

Chapter 6

77 Section 77

The day of the careers fair arrives. It's raining, so you take the bus. Suddenly, you hear your name. You see your friend Amy. 'Hi!' she says. 'How are you?'

'I'm fine,' you say. 'And you?'

'Yeah, I'm fine,' says Amy. 'Did you fix that Facebook problem?'

'Yes, I did,' you say. 'Now I'm going to the university careers fair.'

'Me too!' Amy says. 'I think this careers fair will be a great opportunity. I've got my elevator* chat* ready.'

'Elevator chat? What's that?' you ask.

'Imagine, one day you're in a big company. You get in the elevator. Next to you is a famous businessperson – Bill Gates, for example. You're alone in the elevator with him. You have thirty seconds to tell Bill Gates about yourself. That's the elevator chat.'

'OK, I'll prepare an elevator chat too,' you say.

At the entrance to the careers fair, Amy says, 'Your umbrella's wet. Leave it here and let's go round the fair together.'

Chapter 6

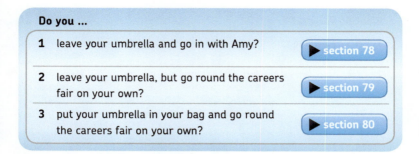

Section 78

Amy walks with you through the careers fair. 'So, Amy,' you say, 'tell me your elevator chat.'

'It's this,' says Amy. 'Excuse me, aren't you the director of Channel 4? My name's Amy Chan and I'm looking for a career in the TV industry. I studied Computer Science at Central University and I also make my own short movies. My videos are all online on my website if you want to have a look. Is there a position for someone like me in your TV company at the moment?'

'That's good,' you say. 'I'll try to think of something similar.'

Suddenly, a man stops to talk to you both. He's older than you. He looks like a company director. 'Amy!' he says.

'Hi, Tom,' says Amy.

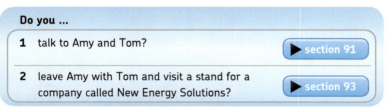

Section 79

There are lots of different companies at the careers fair. There are also some universities. One stand is for the National University. They have free pencils on the stand. You take some.

'Hello,' a man says, 'Are you interested in university courses?'

Chapter 6

What do you say?

1 'Not really. I'm only looking for a job.' ▶ section 83

2 'Yes, I am. I'm interested in anything.' ▶ section 86

80 Section 80

When you enter the careers fair, you see a stand for Movement Limited. It's a famous company. You decide to speak to the woman at the stand. She says 'hello' but she doesn't look friendly. She's looking at your bag – it's very wet.

Do you ...

1 give the woman your elevator chat? ▶ section 84

2 go back and leave your umbrella and bag then talk to her? ▶ section 90

81 Section 81

You look for a security guard. You look for five minutes but you don't find anybody. The thief* escapes. You go back to Tom. 'I'm sorry,' you say.

'It's OK,' says Tom. 'but I need my umbrella. It's raining!' Tom thanks you for your help and then phones a taxi.

▶ section 94

82 Section 82

⭐ You win 1 bonus point. Mark the scorecard on page 115.

Tom Dilger listens to you. 'Very interesting,' he says. 'I don't need any staff* at the moment, but give me your CV. I'll keep it on file.'

'OK,' you say. You give Tom your CV.

44

Chapter 6

'Here's my card,' he says. 'Call me in one or two months. Maybe we'll have some jobs later.' Tom gives you his business card. 'My extension is 215.'

Good decision! Write down the number in the Contacts section on page 115.

Suddenly Tom points to the door. 'Hey!' he shouts. 'That man's got my umbrella and my coat!'

You see a man in the entrance. He has an expensive black coat in his hand and an umbrella in his other hand.

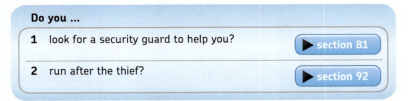

Section 84

Section 83

There are lots of people at the careers fair. You have three options. There are two people at a stand called New Energy Solutions. Nobody is talking to them. Lots of people are waiting to speak to a company called Action 3000. A woman is giving people free T-shirts from one stand. It's called Sports United.

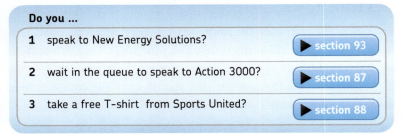

Section 84

The woman listens to your elevator chat. 'Very interesting,' she says. 'Do you have a CV?'

You put your hand in your bag to get a CV, but the paper is wet.

Chapter 6

Your umbrella was very wet and now all your CVs are wet too. You can't give a CV to anyone.

You have nothing to give people at the careers fair.

Bad luck! Your job search ends here.

Go back to the start of the chapter and try again. section 77

85 Section 85

You have a voicemail from Amy on your phone.

'Hi! You won't believe it. I've got an interview with a TV company! I gave them my elevator chat and they loved it! This is amazing. I'm so excited. I'm going home now. Good luck with your job search!'

You speak to some other companies, but you don't find any more interesting job opportunities. You go home. On the way out, you look for your umbrella. It's not there! Maybe someone took it by accident. You go home in the rain.

 section 95

86 Section 86

You talk to the man from the National University for a long time. You tell him about your university course and your job at Pizza Palace. You say it's very difficult to start a career. The man tells you about some interesting courses. He suggests that you do one. The course is free because the government will pay.

What do you say?

1 'No, thank you. I don't want to be a student again.' ▶ section 83

2 'Yes, why not?' ▶ section 89

Chapter 6

Section 87

Action 3000 is a very cool* company. Everyone wants to talk to them. You wait in the queue* for an hour. When you are almost at the front of the queue, your phone rings. You look at your phone and see it's Amy. You decide not to answer, but somebody moves in front of you and starts talking to the people at Action 3000.

'Wait, I was next,' you say.

'Sorry, you have to go to the back of the queue,' says a man from the company.

Bad decision! You wasted* time with Action 3000.

Section 88

You go to the woman at Sports United. She smiles and gives you a T-shirt. You start your elevator chat but the woman stops you. 'I'm sorry,' she says. 'We're not looking for new employees* this year. We're just here to tell people about our company. We make sports kits – shirts for football teams and things like that. If you're interested, you can apply for a job with us next year.'

'Oh,' you say. Next year is no good for you. You need a job this year.

You still have time to talk to one more company. What do you do now?

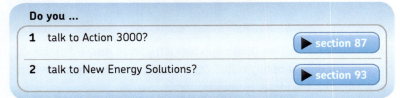

Section 89

You decide to start a new course in September. You work at Pizza Palace until the course starts. You stop looking for a permanent* job and you become a student again.

Your job search ends here, but you do not have your dream job.

47

Chapter 6

You have two options

1 Go back to the start of the chapter and try again. ◀ section 77

2 Go back to the beginning of the maze. Make new decisions. Try to get your dream job! ◀ section 1

90 Section 90

When you return, the woman from Movement Limited is speaking to another person. You give her your CV but she doesn't look very interested. You decide to speak to people from other companies.

▶ section 79

91 Section 91

The man's name is Tom Dilger and he's a friend of Amy's dad. He's the director of a company called ZQ Central Ltd. It is a very modern company with big ideas. It sounds interesting.

Do you ...

1 give Tom Dilger your elevator chat? ▶ section 82

2 leave Tom Dilger and speak to other companies? ▶ section 83

Chapter 6

Section 92

You run outside into the rain. You don't see the thief. He ran too fast. You go back inside. You are very wet.

Tom is smiling. 'Thanks for trying to help,' he says. 'I really appreciate it. Look, I'm sorry we don't we don't have any jobs now at ZQ Central. If there are career* opportunities in the future, I'll call you.' He shakes your hand and walks away.

Section 93

New Energy Solutions are a very friendly company. You talk to a woman called Gupta. She tells you that the company works with green energy. Your mobile phone rings and you look at it. It's Amy, but you decide not to answer it. You talk to Gupta for ten minutes. 'Can I give you my CV?' you say.

'I'm sorry,' says Gupta. 'We only accept online applications. You have to apply on our website.'

'OK,' you say. You feel disappointed, but you made a new contact.

Section 94

You speak to a lot of other companies but you don't find any interesting job opportunities.

Later, you see you have a voicemail on your phone. It's from Amy.

'Hi! You won't believe it. I've got an interview with a TV company! I gave them my elevator chat and they loved it! This is amazing. I'm so excited. I'm going home now. Good luck with your job search!'

You go home. On the way out, you look for your umbrella. It's not there! The thief took your umbrella too! You go home in the rain.

49

Chapter 7

95 Section 95

You're very unhappy. You haven't got any interviews from the companies at the careers fair. You're working full time at Pizza Palace. You spend all your free time looking for jobs. You can't go out with your friends.

One day, you see an advert* for a job at a logistics company. You've got the right qualifications but you aren't sure what 'logistics' means. You look up the word. It means sending and transporting goods. You aren't interested in logistics, but your parents are excited.

'It's a permanent job,' says your dad. 'And you're interested in transport.'

'I like cars – not trucks and cardboard boxes!'

'The pay is much better than at Pizza Palace,' says your mum. 'It's a good company too. It will look good on your CV.'

It's not the type of career* you imagined, but your parents want you to apply.

Do you …

1   decide not to apply for the job and go out with a friend and relax? You need to forget about work.   ▶ section 96

Chapter 7

| 2 | decide not to apply for the job and continue working hard at Pizza Palace? | ▶ section 104 |
| 3 | apply for the job? It's a good opportunity, and you really want to leave Pizza Palace. | ▶ section 108 |

Section 96

You don't apply for the job. Logistics wasn't the right career for you. You call Amy. 'Hi!' she says. She sounds very excited. 'I want to tell you something. It's incredible!'

'What is it?' you ask.

'I had the interview at the TV company this afternoon – I got the job!'

'Wow! That's great news,' you say. 'We must celebrate!'

'Definitely! How about tomorrow night?' she asks.

'That's good for me. We can go to a restaurant.'

'What do you want to eat? Pizza?'

'Ha, ha. Very funny,' you say. 'What about Thai?'

'OK then. Shall we go to the Chiang Mai restaurant? Is 7.30 good for you?'

'Yes, great, see you then.'

Section 97

The dinner at the Chiang Mai restaurant is great. Amy's really happy and you needed a break!

Simon is with you at the restaurant. He's still looking for a job, like you. You talk about your job searches. Amy looked for work for a long time and now she's got a job at a TV company. She always has lots of good advice. She offers to help you.

'Let's talk about it at the weekend. We can go to the Old Town Café. They serve great juice drinks there,' says Amy.

'No!' says Simon. 'Let's go to that new nightclub – the Omega Bar. There's a new DJ on Saturdays, he plays amazing music. I love it there.'

51

Chapter 7

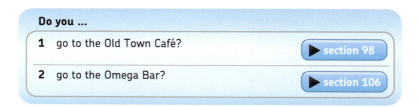

Do you ...
1. go to the Old Town Café? ▶ section 98
2. go to the Omega Bar? ▶ section 106

98 Section 98

You go to the Old Town Café. Amy and Simon sit on a sofa by the window. The café is quiet and you talk about your job search. 'Hey, Simon's got the perfect job for you!' says Amy.

'No, I haven't!' Simon says quickly.

'Yes, you have,' says Amy. 'You know, the web start-up place. What's it called?'

'I can't remember,' says Simon.

'Lava?' asks Amy

'No,' replies Simon. He looks uncomfortable. 'Awaba,' he says.

'It's a strange name,' says Amy. 'Anyway, they're a web start-up company and they're looking for new staff.'

'Really?' you ask. 'What's a web start-up company?'

'They design and build e-commerce* websites,' says Simon. 'If a shop wants a website to sell things online, Awaba can make their website.'

'Oh, it sounds interesting.'

'Maybe,' says Simon.

Chapter 7

'Are you applying for a job at Awaba, Simon?'
'Maybe.'
You stay for a few hours and talk about work and lots of other things.

Section 99

99

Oh, no! Your manager, Ruth, comes back from her lunch break.

'The staff here aren't serving us!' a customer complains. 'What's happening?'

Ruth sees you with Amy and Simon. You start working again quickly. Later, she says, 'I saw you with your friends. We were really busy today! You can't chat* to your friends on busy days. It isn't fair to the other staff.'

'I'm sorry,' you say. 'It won't happen again.'

After work, you call Amy and Simon. You arrange to meet them on Friday evening.

Section 100

100

The next day, you Google 'Awaba'. The website is amazing and the company looks interesting. There are lots of job opportunities, not just for programmers. You decide to apply for an office job.

A week later, you get an email from Awaba. It's good news. You send a message to Amy.

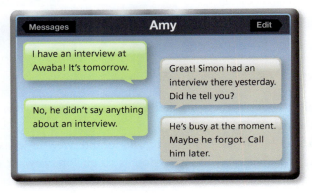

53

Chapter 7

You call Simon. 'Sorry, my phone was broken,' he says. 'I didn't have your number. The interview? Easy. They were very friendly. Very relaxed. Everyone wears jeans and T-shirts, so don't wear formal* clothes for the interview.'

'Really?' you ask.

'Really,' he says.

101 Section 101

⭐ You win 1 bonus point. Mark the scorecard on page 115.

You arrive at Awaba and a receptionist takes you to the interview room. Two directors of the company interview you. It's a good interview and they are very friendly.

The man's wearing a suit*, and the woman's wearing very formal clothes. Through the window you can see that the programmers and designers are wearing jeans and T-shirts. Wearing smart* clothes was the right choice.

102 Section 102

After three months, DistroTrans offer you a permanent* contract*.

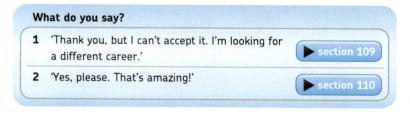

103 Section 103

You talk to your parents about the interview. You tell them what Simon said.

'No,' says your dad. 'You can't go to an interview in jeans and a T-shirt! You always wear smart clothes to an interview. It doesn't matter what they wear at Awaba. You aren't working there yet.'

Chapter 7

> **Do you ...**
> 1 wear smart clothes?   ▶ section 101
> 2 wear jeans and a T-shirt?   ▶ section 111

Section 104

You turn on the radio to listen to the news. There's an interview with a businessman.

'Why is it difficult for people to get their first job?'

'Companies prefer to give jobs to people who *have* a job. If you haven't got a job, we aren't interested.'

'Why not?'

'Because a person with a job is more successful than a person without a job. And I only want successful people in my company!'

'That's silly! You can't get a job without experience and you can't get experience without a job. So how can people get their *first* job?'

'I don't care. It's not my problem.'

You have a job. It's only a job at Pizza Palace, but that is better than no job.

▶ section 105

Section 105

You're having a bad day at work. There aren't enough staff*. The customers have to wait a long time. They aren't happy and they complain a lot. Sometimes they're rude. There's a notice in the kitchen:

> **BE POLITE!**
> The customer is always right

You feel terrible. You work long hours and some customers are difficult. Then the job search takes all your free time. Suddenly, Amy

55

Chapter 7

and Simon walk into the restaurant. 'You don't look very happy. Let's go for a coffee,' says Amy.

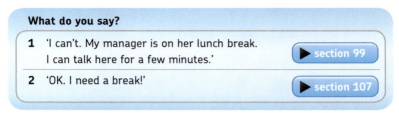

What do you say?

1 'I can't. My manager is on her lunch break. I can talk here for a few minutes.' ▶ section 99

2 'OK. I need a break!' ▶ section 107

106 Section 106

You arrive at the Omega Bar and meet Amy, but Simon isn't there. The music is very loud and you don't hear your phone ring. Later you look at your mobile and see you have a voicemail.

'Err, hi. It's me, Simon. Look, I can't come tonight. I have to do something else. So have a good time. Err, bye.'

The music in the Omega Bar is great. You have a fun evening with Amy, but there's one problem – the nightclub's very noisy. You can shout, but you can't talk. You don't get any careers advice*.

Bad luck! Your job search ends here.

Go back to the start of the chapter and try again. ◀ section 95

107 Section 107

You walk out of Pizza Palace with Amy and Simon. Immediately, you see Ruth, your manager.

'Are you OK?' she asks. 'Where are you going?'

'I'm sorry,' you say. 'I don't feel well. I need to get some air.'

'Oh dear, I hope you're OK. Have a rest and come back when you feel better.'

'Thanks, Ruth. I'll be OK. I'll come back in half an hour,' you say.

You go to a café with Amy and Simon.

▶ section 98

56

Chapter 7

Section 108

You phone the number in the advert. The secretary asks you to wait, and then you speak to the manager. She explains the job and the pay, and she asks you about your work experience. They're looking for five new members of staff and she offers you a job immediately. It's a temporary* contract. You'll work there for twelve weeks.

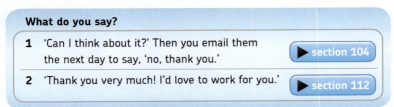

What do you say?

1 'Can I think about it?' Then you email them the next day to say, 'no, thank you.' ▶ section 104

2 'Thank you very much! I'd love to work for you.' ▶ section 112

Section 109

'Thank you for being honest,' says your manager. 'We'll offer the contract to someone else. You're a good member of staff and we like you. I'll recommend your work on LinkedIn.'

You call Ruth at Pizza Palace. 'Are there any positions at the moment?' you ask.

'Yes!' laughs Ruth. 'There's always a position for you! I'll call you on Monday to talk about shifts.'

'That's brilliant. Thanks very much, Ruth.'

▶ section 104

Section 110

Working at DistroTrans isn't your dream job, but the money is good and the work is more interesting. Life is good. You buy a car and you move into your own flat. Your job search ends here.

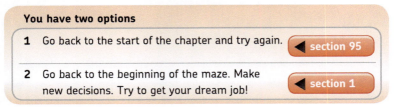

You have two options

1 Go back to the start of the chapter and try again. ◀ section 95

2 Go back to the beginning of the maze. Make new decisions. Try to get your dream job! ◀ section 1

Chapter 7

111 Section 111

You arrive at Awaba and a receptionist takes you to the interview room. Two directors of the company interview you. The man's wearing a suit*, and the woman's wearing very formal clothes. Through the window, you see that the programmers and designers are wearing jeans and T-shirts. The interviewers are friendly but the interview only lasts fifteen minutes.

'Why didn't I wear smart clothes?' you think. 'And why did Simon tell me to wear casual* clothes?'

112 Section 112

The next Monday, you start work at DistroTrans, the logistics company. The work is easy and the staff are friendly. You're happy. It's much nicer than Pizza Palace, but it isn't the career you want. You work 9.00 a.m. – 5.00 p.m. and you aren't tired in the evenings. You can look for jobs and go out with friends.

Chapter 8

Section 113

One morning you see you have a voicemail on your mobile phone. Maybe it's from Awaba. You're very excited!

'Hi, this is James Green, HR Director at Awaba. We wanted to thank you for coming for the interview last week. There were a lot of very good applicants* for the positions on offer. Unfortunately, you weren't successful on this occasion. We wish you good luck in your job search for the future.'

You feel unhappy. After the careers fair, Amy got a job at a TV company. Mark works for a newspaper. You still don't have a job.

You text Simon to find out about his interview. He replies immediately.

Suddenly, your phone rings. It's Mark. 'I need your help!' he says.

Section 114

'What's wrong?' you ask

'It's work,' Mark says. 'In next week's newspaper, we have a two-page story about cycling in the countryside.'

'OK.'

'Some local cyclists agreed to do a cycle ride and appear in some photos. Now, they can't do it. Everyone in the cycle group has the flu*. Please, please, will you come on a cycling trip with me? Your photo will be in the newspaper!'

'OK, Mark. No problem! I'll do it,' you say.

'Thanks so much!' he says. 'Amy is coming too. Simon isn't coming. He's busy.'

Chapter 8

115 Section 115

It is the day of the cycle ride and Mark's very pleased to see you. 'Thanks so much!' he says. 'We'll cycle for twenty kilometres. The newspaper's photographer will take pictures.'

It's a cold day, but it's also sunny. It feels good to be on a bike. Your group leaves the city. You cycle into the hills. The other cyclists are faster than you and Mark. They are at the top of the hill when you are at the bottom.

You look at Mark. His face is red. The photographer takes his picture. He looks terrible. 'My legs hurt!' he says. 'I hate cycling.'

'Come on!' shouts Amy, from the top of the hill. 'We're waiting for you!' The photographer takes her photo. She's smiling and she looks great. Finally, you stop for lunch. While you're eating your sandwiches, Amy comes to speak to you. 'I want to show you something.' She gives you her phone and shows you a photo of a cat.

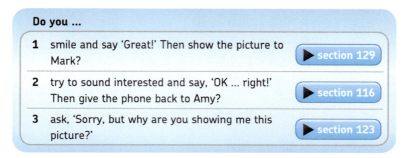

Do you ...

1	smile and say 'Great!' Then show the picture to Mark?	▶ section 129
2	try to sound interested and say, 'OK ... right!' Then give the phone back to Amy?	▶ section 116
3	ask, 'Sorry, but why are you showing me this picture?'	▶ section 123

Chapter 8

Section 116

Amy doesn't look at the phone again. She puts it in her bag. 'Oh, sorry,' she says. 'I thought it was interesting.' Amy doesn't speak to you again.

One of the other cyclists, Dave, sits next to you. 'I hear you work at Pizza Palace,' Dave says. 'I work for Kebab Centre and we need a new assistant manager. Do you want to work with us? Kebab Centre pays more money than Pizza Palace.'

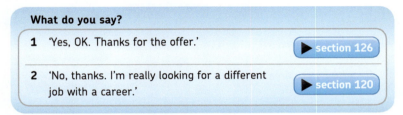

What do you say?

1 'Yes, OK. Thanks for the offer.' ▶ section 126

2 'No, thanks. I'm really looking for a different job with a career.' ▶ section 120

Section 117

'Do you want to work with us?' asks Gary. 'If you say 'yes' now, you will go with a person from the office and watch them at work.'

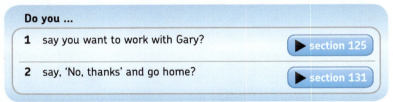

Do you ...

1 say you want to work with Gary? ▶ section 125

2 say, 'No, thanks' and go home? ▶ section 131

Section 118

You show her the phone.

'Oh! Sorry,' Amy says, 'that was a mistake. That's a photo of my cat. I didn't want to show you that. I wanted to show you a job advert*.'

▶ section 121

Section 119

The next day, you phone Gary. 'Could you tell me about the advertising* job, please?' you say.

Chapter 8

'Well, we go to people's houses,' says Gary. 'We tell them about local businesses, like restaurants. If they're interested, we give them a special offer, so people use that local business.'

'How does it work?' you ask.

'For example, we can offer a meal at a restaurant at a special price. If we give people a 20% discount for dinner, they'll go and eat at the restaurant. Then they'll tell their friends about it.'

You're disappointed. This is not a real advertising job.

120 Section 120

'OK, it's your decision,' says Dave. You continue cycling. It's a very nice day and the countryside is beautiful. The photographer takes lots of pictures.

You help Mark, but you also have a fun day. At the end, Mark thanks everyone. 'Remember to look in the newspaper this weekend,' he says. 'This is your fifteen minutes of fame*!'

You say goodbye and go home. It's time to start your job search again.

121 Section 121

Amy touches the screen and shows you a job advert.

Chapter 8

Do you ...

1. phone Gary to ask about the job? ▶ section 119
2. go to the interview on Wednesday? ▶ section 122

Section 122

You go to the interview. The office is in a very old building. There are seven other people there for the interview. A man says, 'hello'. He's about forty years old and he's wearing an old suit*. You notice his socks – they're different colours.

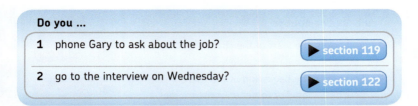

'Er ... hi everyone, I'm Gary,' he says. 'Er ... this is an advertising company. We do our advertising differently. We don't put adverts in newspapers or on TV. We go to people's houses. We tell them about our customers, like local restaurants. If they're interested, we arrange a special price for the people. For example, 20% off a meal.' The man sniffs. 'This is how we do our advertising.'

▶ section 117

Section 123

'This is a great way to make money,' says Amy.

'Really?' you ask. You look again at the photo of the cat.

'Yes, it's a job opportunity.'

'I'm not sure,' you say. 'I don't want to work with animals.'

'Animals?' asks Amy. 'What are you talking about?'

▶ section 118

Section 124

'Good,' says Gary. He shakes your hand. 'Welcome to the team!'

You leave Pizza Palace and you start your new job in advertising. You have a job, but it isn't your dream job.

63

Chapter 8

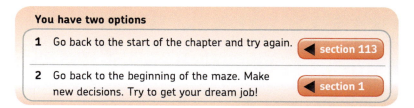

Section 125

Only you accept the offer. The other people leave. Gary says, 'OK, you'll work with me today. Follow me.'

You walk out of the office to Gary's car. Gary drives to lots of different houses. He talks to lots of people. At every house, he says the same thing. 'Hello, don't worry, we're not politicians. We're here to tell you about some local businesses. We can offer you a special price on things like meals in restaurants.' People aren't very friendly to Gary. Some people don't open the door. One man shouts at you.

At the end, Gary says, 'It was a difficult morning. But I like you, and I want to work with you. If you want to work in my advertising company, I have a job for you.'

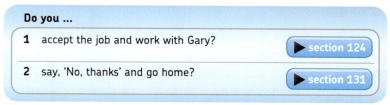

Section 126

You leave your job at Pizza Palace and you start work at Kebab Centre. It's a friendly restaurant and you enjoy working with Dave. Your new boss is nice and the food is good. You get free meals every day.

Unfortunately, after one month Pizza Palace buys Kebab Centre. You are working for the same company again!

Bad luck! Your job search ends here.

Go back to the start of the chapter and try again. ◀ section 113

Chapter 8

Section 127

When you get home, you look at some job websites. There is only one new job advert:

Do you want to work in advertising?

We are looking for young people to work in advertising. If you have a university degree, come to our office on Wednesday 25th at 9.00 am for an interview.

If you have any questions, phone Gary at **Word of Mouth Connections** on 07700 900113.

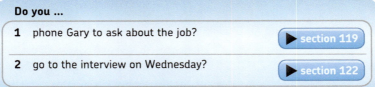

Do you ...

1 phone Gary to ask about the job? ▶ section 119

2 go to the interview on Wednesday? ▶ section 122

Section 128

⭐ You win 1 bonus point. Mark the scorecard on page 115.

Good decision! It's not a good idea to go to every job interview. You need a day to visit the company and you also have to work at Pizza Palace.

'I'm sorry,' you say. 'Actually, I am looking for another kind of job.'
'That's OK,' says Gary. 'Good luck with your job search.'

▶ section 131

Section 129

Mark looks at the phone. 'This is a picture of your cat,' he says.

'Is it? Sorry!' says Amy. Everyone laughs. 'That was a mistake,' she says. 'I really wanted to show you a job offer.'

▶ section 121

Chapter 8

130 Section 130

The office is in a very old building. There are seven other people at the interview. Gary is there too, the boss of Word of Mouth Connections. He's about forty years old and he's wearing an old suit*. You notice his socks – they're different colours. Gary remembers your phone call and he says 'hello'.

Then he explains about the company again to all the job candidates. Finally, he looks at you.

 section 117

Chapter 9

Section 131

The next day, you are working at Pizza Palace when your boss wants to speak to you. You're a bit worried. Ruth was really friendly to you six months ago, but now she's different. 'Why do you always have time off work?' Ruth asks.

'I need to do things,' you reply. 'I need to organise my life.'

'Why do you need to organise your life?'

'I, er ...'

'Listen, I know what you're doing. You're looking for jobs. You're going for interviews.'

'But ...'

'But nothing! I'm talking! You come here with your university degree* and you think you're so clever*. You think you have all the answers.'

'I don't ...'

'I *know* you don't have all the answers!' laughs Ruth. 'This is your final warning*. You can work all your shifts, or you can leave. Then you'll have lots of time to look for a career!'

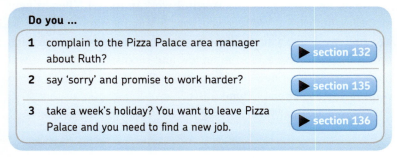

Do you ...

1 complain to the Pizza Palace area manager about Ruth? ▶ section 132

2 say 'sorry' and promise to work harder? ▶ section 135

3 take a week's holiday? You want to leave Pizza Palace and you need to find a new job. ▶ section 136

Section 132

Ruth is being unfair. You're sure the Pizza Palace area manager* can help you. You arrange a meeting with him. He tells you to meet him the next day in Ruth's office.

Chapter 9

The next day, you knock on the door and walk into the office. The area manager's in the office but Ruth isn't. 'Sit down,' he says, but he doesn't look at you. After a few minutes, he looks up. He doesn't smile. He listens to your problem, but he doesn't say anything. Then Ruth comes in. They shake hands and smile.

'Hi, Nigel. Is your son better?' Ruth asks.

'Yes, he's fine now, thank you,' replies the area manager. 'How's your husband?'

'Great, thanks.'

They talk for a few minutes. You realise that they're friends. Then the area manager asks you, 'Where do you see yourself in five years?'

Do you ...

1. tell the truth about your job search and say, 'In five years, I'll have a great job somewhere else'?

2. lie and say, 'I want to be at Pizza Palace in five years. I love it here. I'm going to work all my shifts and be a good employee'?

133 Section 133

When you get home, there's a voicemail message on your phone.

'Hello, my name's Joanna Werth. I work in the HR* department at Cyclox Industries. We received your job application a few weeks ago and we'd like you to come to the first stage of the selection process*. You'll have a short interview and successful candidates will have a second interview on another day. Please can you ring me to confirm you can attend? Thanks. Bye.'

You ring Joanna Werth and say you can come to the interview.

134 Section 134

The area manager says, 'You don't work all your shifts, but you're a good worker. You're telling the truth, too – I like that. I want you to stay, but don't go to interviews when you have a shift here.'

68

Chapter 9

Section 135

135

You work very hard. Ruth watches you all the time. You can't make any personal phone calls or send text messages while you're working. Simon usually calls you a lot, so you text him.

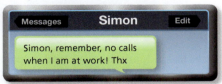

One day, you're at work when your phone rings. You don't know the number. It might be a company phoning you about a job interview.

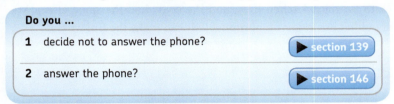

Section 136

136

You feel very happy because you aren't working at Pizza Palace for one week. You've got lots of time for your job search.

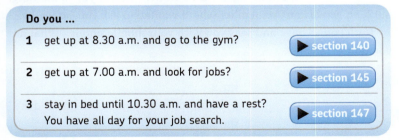

Section 137

137

You and Darren shake hands. Darren smiles, and you smile too. 'We saved the restaurant!' you say.

'Yes, but it was frightening!' says Darren. 'You acted quickly. I was lucky. Thank you.'

Chapter 9

Ruth called the fire service but when they arrive, everything's OK. The restaurant continues as normal.

When you go home that night, you feel very tired and you sleep well.

138 Section 138

⭐ You win 1 bonus point. Mark the scorecard on page 115.
Your boss ran away, but you showed leadership* and you didn't panic. Well done!

You made a good decision about the fire. You should use a damp cloth for most kitchen fires, and the coats had the same effect. You shouldn't use water on burning oil. It can make the fire worse.

139 Section 139

You don't answer the phone, but Ruth still isn't happy. 'Keep your phone on silent when you're at work,' she says. 'This is not the place for personal phone calls.'

She leaves and you look at your phone. There's a voicemail.

'Er, hi. It's me, Simon again. Er, I wanted to ask you something, but I, er. Now I can't remember what I wanted to ask you, so, er, bye.'

Ruth comes back and sees you with your mobile phone. 'What are you doing?' she asks.

'Er, I'm putting my phone on silent,' you say.

Ruth looks at you. 'Your hat is dirty,' she says.

You take off your hat and look at it. 'It's clean,' you say.

Ruth takes your hat and drops it on the floor. 'Now it's dirty!' she laughs. The floor is wet and she puts her foot on it. 'Go and get a clean hat.'

70

Chapter 9

Do you ...

1. get a clean hat? You don't like Ruth, but you don't say anything. ▶ section 142
2. say, 'That was stupid! I hate this job. I can't work here anymore. Goodbye.' ▶ section 144

Section 140

140

You go to the gym. Afterwards, you feel fresh and full of energy. Good choice.

In the afternoons, you apply for some jobs and you have lots of rest. After one week you feel ready to go back to Pizza Palace.

▶ section 142

Section 141

141

You continue your job search but you don't go to interviews when you have shifts at Pizza Palace. Ruth is nicer to you, and the area manager is friendly when he visits the restaurant.

▶ section 142

Section 142

142

One afternoon, you walk into the kitchen. Darren, the chef, is making chips. 'Can I have a chip?' you ask.

'No, sorry, they aren't ready yet.'

Ruth walks in. 'What are you talking about?'

'Oh, nothing,' says Darren. You smile at him.

71

Chapter 9

Suddenly, there is a 'BANG'. Flames go from the cooker right up to the ceiling. 'Fire! Help, help!' screams Ruth. She runs out of the kitchen.

You look at the fire and at Darren. He looks scared*. Only you can put out the fire. You see a big pan* of water and also your workmates' coats on the door.

Section 143

You pick up the pan of water. Unfortunately, you shouldn't use water on burning oil. It can make the fire worse!

'Stop! Don't do that!' Darren shouts. 'There's a fire extinguisher* over there.'

You use the fire extinguisher to put out the fire.

Section 144

Now you don't have a job at Pizza Palace, but you don't have your dream job.

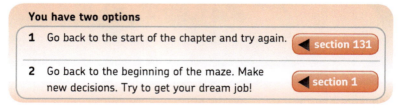

Section 145

You have a healthy breakfast and you plan your day. You apply for some jobs and you have lots of rest.

Chapter 9

After one week you feel ready to go back to Pizza Palace.

 section 142

Section 146

It's Simon again! 'Don't call me at work!' you shout loudly.

Ruth hears you talking on your phone. She sacks* you. You lose your job.

Bad luck! Your job search ends here.

Go back to the start of the chapter and try again. section 131

Section 147

It's nice to have a rest, but remember that a job search is the same as a job. You need to get up on time, eat well, take exercise, and work hard every day.

Bad luck! Your job search ends here.

Go back to the start of the chapter and try again. section 131

Section 148

'So, do you really want to be here in five years?' asks the area manager.

'Yes,' you say.

'That's not true,' says Ruth. 'You're looking for another job. You want a better career and you sometimes use Pizza Palace time for your job search.'

The area manager talks to Ruth about your situation. Then he tells you to leave the company.

Bad luck! Your job search ends here.

Go back to the start of the chapter and try again. section 131

Chapter 10

149 Section 149

It's the day of the interview. You arrive early and you have time for a coffee before you go into the offices. When you arrive, you meet Joanna Werth at reception. 'Hi. Welcome to Cyclox Industries,' she says.

'Thank you,' you say. 'I'm looking forward to the interview.'

'That's good,' says Joanna. 'Actually, today, we'll just have a chat* with you. Before your interview, we'd like you to do a quick test for us.'

'Oh? What kind of test?' you say.

'It's a reasoning test. It shows us how you think. All the candidates* are doing it,' says Joanna.

'How many other candidates are there for the job?' you ask.

'Oh, about 60,' says Joanna. She opens a door and you enter a very big room. Lots of people are sitting at computers. You look around. The other candidates are all doing the test.

Do you ...

1	sit down and do the test?	▶ section 150
2	continue the conversation with Joanna?	▶ section 151
3	refuse to do the test?	▶ section 152

Chapter 10

Section 150

'Do you have everything you need to do the test?' asks Joanna.

'Yes, thank you,' you say.

'OK, well, good luck!' Joanna says with a smile. She looks at her watch, then she leaves you.

You look at the computer and you start the test.

Section 151

'Why do you give this test to candidates?' you ask.

'It's a good way to find the best people,' says Joanna. 'In the test, companies learn about a person's intelligence. The test is different to the interview. In the interview, companies learn about a person's personality.'

Joanna looks at her watch.

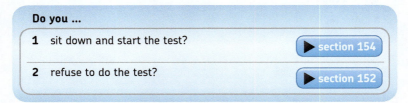

Section 152

'I'm sorry,' you say. 'I'm here for a job interview. I don't want to do this test.'

Joanna looks surprised. 'All our candidates take the test. Are you sure you don't want to do it?'

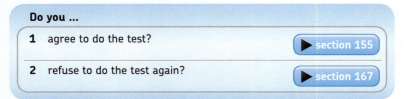

Chapter 10

Section 153

That's correct. Next question.

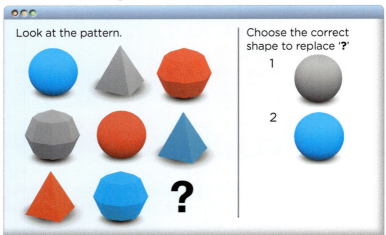

Do you choose ...

1	Answer 1?	▶ section 157
2	Answer 2?	▶ section 163

Section 154

You read the first question.

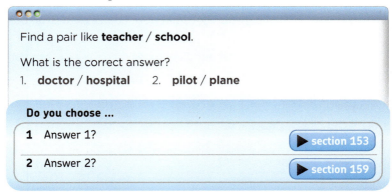

Chapter 10

Section 155

'Good, I was worried for a moment!' says Joanna. 'Please sit here. You have 30 minutes to complete the test.'

Section 156

That's correct.

Section 157

That's correct. Next question.

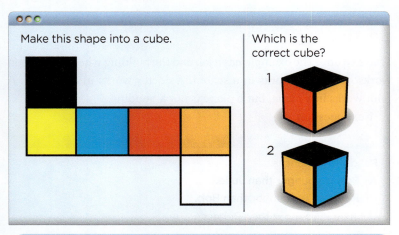

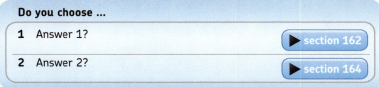

Chapter 10

158 Section 158

Next question.

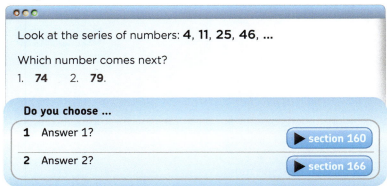

Look at the series of numbers: **4**, **11**, **25**, **46**, ...

Which number comes next?
1. **74**   2. **79**.

Do you choose ...
1 Answer 1? ▶ section 160
2 Answer 2? ▶ section 166

159 Section 159

That's wrong. The example has a job and the building where the person works. A teacher works in a school. A doctor works in a hospital. A pilot works in a plane, but a plane is not a building.

Next question.

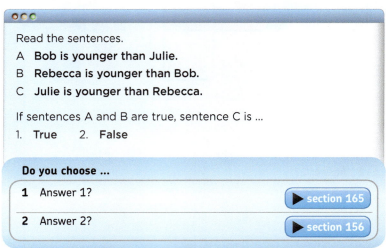

Read the sentences.
A **Bob is younger than Julie.**
B **Rebecca is younger than Bob.**
C **Julie is younger than Rebecca.**

If sentences A and B are true, sentence C is ...
1. **True**   2. **False**

Do you choose ...
1 Answer 1? ▶ section 165
2 Answer 2? ▶ section 156

Chapter 10

Section 160

That's correct.

Joanna looks at your test results. 'OK,' she said 'you got some answers right but you got some answers wrong. I think your test is OK.'

She chats to you for a short time about your life. You tell her about your studies and your job at Pizza Palace. 'That's very interesting,' she says. 'We'll contact you if you get a second interview. Thanks for coming today.'

You say 'goodbye' and leave the company. You don't feel good about your test result, but maybe you have a chance.

 section 168

Section 161

Joanna comes to look at your test results. You got lots of wrong answers. You say 'goodbye' to Joanna and you return to your job at Pizza Palace.

Your test was not a success* and the company does not ask you to come back for a second interview.

Bad luck! Your job search ends here.

Go back to the start of the chapter and try again. ◀ section 149

Section 162

⭐ You win 1 bonus point. Mark the scorecard on page 115.
That's correct! You got all the answers right.

Joanna comes to look at your test results. You leave the room together. She chats to you for a short time about your life. You tell her about your studies and your job at Pizza Palace.

'Thanks for coming,' she says with a smile. 'We'll contact you if you get a second interview.'

This part of the interview process is finished.

 section 168

Chapter 10

163 Section 163

That's wrong. Each column has one example of each shape and each shape is a different colour.

The correct answer is:

▶ section 158

164 Section 164

Wrong answer. The correct cube was this one:

▶ section 158

165 Section 165

That's wrong.

The order of ages is:

Oldest	Julie
↓	Bob
Youngest	Rebecca

So sentence C is false. Rebecca is younger than Julie.

▶ section 161

166 Section 166

That's wrong.

4, 11, 25, 46, ...

This is a Fibonacci sequence based on the 7 times table.

4 + (7x1) = 11

11 + (7x2) = 25

25 + (7x3) = 46.

So the next number is 46 + (7x4) = 74.

▶ section 161

Chapter 10

Section 167

'I did lots of exams at school. I have a degree* from university. Why do you want me to do more tests?'

'I understand,' says Joanna. 'Thank you for your time.'

You leave the company and return to work at Pizza Palace. This was your last opportunity to get a good job and you did not succeed.

Bad luck! Your job search ends here.

Go back to the start of the chapter and try again. section 149

Chapter 11

168 Section 168

You've got a voicemail on your phone. Maybe it's about the interview and the test.

'Good afternoon. It's Joanna Werth here, from Cyclox Industries. I'm calling about the interview you had last week. Your test results were good and we'd like to see you again for a second interview. This interview will be a group task* and it will last about half a day. So, well done, and we're looking forward to seeing you again.'

You call Amy. 'What's a 'group task interview'?' you ask.

'Oh, that's good news. It's expensive for companies to organise group tasks. They obviously liked you in your first interview.'

'Why is it expensive?'

'Because they need an organiser and one or two other people. The organiser explains the tasks. The other people watch the candidates*. They're looking for people with good teamwork skills*. Employers* don't want bossy* staff* and they don't want shy* staff. Just be yourself. You'll be fine!'

> **Do you ...**
>
> 1 do some research into Cyclox Industries? 'Knowledge is power,' you remember Simon saying. ▶ section 169
>
> 2 prepare some information to say about yourself? 'Preparation is the key,' you remember Mark saying. ▶ section 174
>
> 3 prepare yourself physically for the group task? 'You are what you eat,' you remember Amy saying. ▶ section 178

169 Section 169

The day before the interview, you visit the Cyclox Industries website and read all of its pages. You read the Wikipedia page about Cyclox

Industries and you discover some interesting facts about the company. Some of the information is negative. Then you Google 'Cyclox Industries'. People say good and bad things about the company. Finally, you read financial reports about the company. In the end, you're tired, but you know a lot about Cyclox Industries!

On the morning of the interview, you check your email. There's a newsletter from a job search website.

It's too late to prepare some personal information now. You take the bus to Cyclox Industries and think about basic information you can give.

Section 170

Three more people walk into reception. They're here for the interview. They start chatting. You decide to listen to their stories.

Section 171

Now there are eight people in reception, including Joanna Werth.

A man with a nice suit* and grey hair says, 'Hi. Thank you all for coming today. My name's John Goodman. I'm organising today's interview. We have six candidates this morning. Please follow me to the interview room.'

John Goodman assessed* the candidates in reception. 'Oh, no!' you think. 'I talked a lot and I didn't ask the other candidates any questions!'

Chapter 11

172 Section 172

You arrive at Cyclox Industries and go into reception. You see Joanna Werth. 'Hi, Joanna,' you say with a smile.

'Welcome back,' she says. 'Help yourself to coffee. The group task will start in 20 minutes.'

There are three other people in reception. Maybe they are there for the group task interview. On the other hand, Cyclox Industries has a lot of visitors. Maybe they aren't there for the interview.

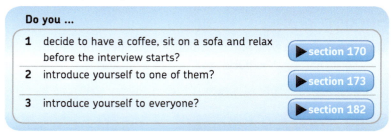

Do you ...
1. decide to have a coffee, sit on a sofa and relax before the interview starts? ▶ section 170
2. introduce yourself to one of them? ▶ section 173
3. introduce yourself to everyone? ▶ section 182

173 Section 173

'Are you here for the interview?' you ask.

'Yes,' the candidate replies. 'Are you?'

'Yes. Tell me about yourself,' you say.

A man with a nice suit* and grey hair comes in and says, 'Hi, I'm John.' He listens to the conversation and smiles.

Chapter 11

Section 174

174

Good choice! You Google 'group task interview'.

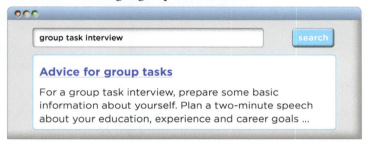

You decide to add some personal information to your elevator chat. You think about how the job at Cyclox Industries will help you to achieve your goals. You practise your speech with Amy and Mark. They think it's brilliant.

You take the bus to Cyclox Industries. You feel confident* and happy.

▶ section 172

Section 175

175

You and your partner ask and answer questions about yourselves. It's fun. Then John says, 'OK, stop. Now tell me about your partners.'

The other pairs are very good. They give a lot of interesting information. Your turn is good too. You're a bit nervous but you both give the correct information. John smiles and says, 'Well done.'

▶ section 183

Section 176

176

'Cards aren't the same as Lego!' says one candidate.

'I've got an idea,' says another candidate. 'Let's make a triangle and put a card on top. That's a good start.'

'No, no, wait!' you say. 'Give me the cards. I'll show you how to make a room with four walls.' They give you the cards and you make a room with four walls. It falls over. 'Who moved the table?' you ask.

'No one moved the table!' says one of the candidates. 'Your house

Chapter 11

fell over because it wasn't a very good design.'

'Listen!' you say. Then you forget what you wanted to say. John is looking at you. He doesn't look pleased. You feel very hot. In the end, the group makes the house while you direct.

After 45 minutes, there's a small card house on the table.

 section 180

177 Section 177

Now there are eight people in reception, including Joanna Werth.

A man with a nice suit* and grey hair says, 'Hi. Thank you all for coming today. My name's John Goodman. I'm organising today's interview. We have six candidates this morning. Please follow me to the interview room.'

John Goodman assessed the candidates in reception. 'Oh, no!' you think. 'I wasn't very friendly! I didn't say anything.'

 section 179

178 Section 178

When you aren't working at Pizza Palace, you try to take care of yourself. You go to the gym and you eat healthy food. You feel relaxed, happy and confident.

On the morning of the interview, you check your email. There's a newsletter from a job search website.

It's too late to prepare some personal information now. You take the bus to Cyclox Industries and think about the basic information you can give.

 section 172

Chapter 11

Section 179

'Please sit down,' says John Goodman. 'There are two tasks* this morning. For the first task, I want you to speak to the person next to you. Then tell the group about your partner. Does everyone understand? Good. You have five minutes.'

You look at your partner.

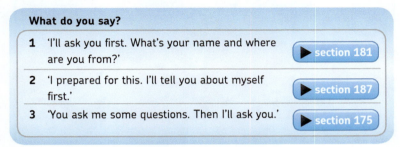

What do you say?		
1	'I'll ask you first. What's your name and where are you from?'	▶ section 181
2	'I prepared for this. I'll tell you about myself first.'	▶ section 187
3	'You ask me some questions. Then I'll ask you.'	▶ section 175

Section 180

'Thanks, everyone, and well done!' says John Goodman. 'The successful candidate will get an email in the next ten days. Good luck!'

▶ section 185

Section 181

You ask your partner lots of questions. It's very interesting and your partner is funny. You both laugh. Then you remember the time. There's only one minute left. You can't tell your partner much about yourself before John says, 'OK, stop. Now tell me about your partners.'

The other pairs are very good. They give a lot of interesting information. Your turn isn't great because your partner doesn't know anything about you. John doesn't look pleased.

▶ section 183

Section 182

You tell them some personal information about yourself. Then some more people come in.

87

Chapter 11

'Hi. Are you all here for the interview?' you ask.

'Yes,' they say. You are pleased because they seem quite shy.

 section 171

183 Section 183

'Now it's time for your second task this morning,' says John Goodman. 'I want you all to sit at this table. On the table there are three packs of cards. I want you to build a house using the cards. Does everyone understand?'

'Do you want a big house?' asks a candidate.

'It doesn't matter. Just build me a house.'

'How long have we got?'

'Good question,' says John Goodman. 'About 45 minutes.'

Two women walk into the room. 'These are my colleagues*. They are helping me to assess* this part of the interview.'

What do you do?	
1	Open a pack of cards and say, 'I was brilliant at Lego when I was a kid. I know how to make this house really strong.' ▶ section 176
2	Say, 'I don't know how to make a house from cards. Any ideas anyone?' ▶ section 184
3	Offer the packs of cards to the other candidates and say, 'How shall we start? Is anyone good at making houses from cards?' ▶ section 188

Chapter 11

Section 184

184

Two of the candidates think they have the best ideas. You don't want an argument*, so you don't say anything. The other candidates decide what to do. You think it's better to be polite and not argue*.

Slowly, your group builds a small house from the cards. It isn't very strong. Everyone's working quietly except the two bossy* candidates. John Goodman says, 'I want a garage next to my house.'

You can see a few good places for a garage, but so can everyone else.
'Here!' says one.
'No,' says another. 'There isn't enough space there.'

You don't want another argument, so you move to the other side of the table and you build a different part of the house.

After 45 minutes, there is a small card house on the table.

Section 185

185

You go home and think about the interview task. You decide you did well. After just two days, you get another email from Cyclox Industries. You're very excited!

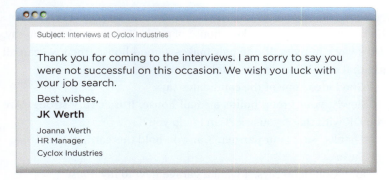

You're very disappointed*. You call Amy. 'Never mind,' she says. 'It's very useful to have interview practice.'

Chapter 11

186 Section 186

Now there are eight people in reception, including Joanna Werth.

John says, 'Hi. Thank you all for coming today. My name's John Goodman. I'm organising today's interview. We have six candidates this morning. Please follow me to the interview room.'

John Goodman assessed the candidates in reception. 'Good,' you think. 'I was friendly! I didn't talk too much and I didn't stay quiet.'

 section 179

187 Section 187

You tell your partner all about yourself. Your partner doesn't say anything. You look at your watch. You took four minutes. Your partner is telling you their personal information when John says, 'OK. Stop. Now tell me about your partners.'

The other pairs are very good. They give a lot of interesting information. Your turn's a disaster because you don't know anything about your partner. Your partner's annoyed*. John doesn't look pleased.

 section 183

188 Section 188

⭐ You win 1 bonus point. Mark the scorecard on page 115.

No one knows how to make a house of cards. 'I have an idea,' you say. 'Let's work in pairs. If one pair makes a good house, then we can all use that one. What do you think?'

'Good idea,' one of the candidates says.

Slowly, your group builds a small house. It isn't very strong. 'Are you OK with that?' you ask. 'Can I help you?'

'Thanks,' says your partner. 'Can you hold this card, please?'
'Sure.'

John Goodman says, 'I want a garage next to my house.'

'OK. Where shall we put it?' you ask your group.

'What about next to this wall?' says someone.

'Yes, that's a great idea!' you say. John Goodman smiles at you. After 45 minutes, there's a small card house on the table.

 section 180

Chapter 12

Section 189

You wake up on Friday morning. It's a beautiful day. It's sunny and warm. Today you have an afternoon shift at Pizza Palace. 'I'll go for walk,' you think. Suddenly, your mobile rings. It's your friend, Amy. 'Hi, Amy,' you say. 'How are you?'

'Not good,' says Amy. 'I have a big problem at work!' Amy's working on a chat show* at a TV station. The chat show is on TV every day 3.00–4.00 p.m. On the show there are interviews with special guests. There are usually 60 people in the audience* and they can ask questions too.

'Every day, I have to find the audience,' Amy says. 'Usually it's the same people. We have a list and I ask them to come to the show by phone or email. Some days it's easy to find 60 people, but today I only have 20 people! If I don't find some more people, I'll lose my job! Can you be in the audience for my show this afternoon? Please, please come and help me!'

'But Amy, I have a shift at Pizza Palace this afternoon,' you say.

'This is important for me. And maybe for you too, because the guests on today's show are all businesspeople. You can meet some of them, and maybe give them your elevator chat.'

There's a problem. You can't go on the TV show and work at Pizza Palace. The show's at the same time as your Pizza Palace shift.

Chapter 12

> **Do you ...**
> 1 agree to help Amy and phone Ruth at Pizza Palace and tell her the truth? ▶ section 199
> 2 agree to help Amy and phone Ruth at Pizza Palace and you say you are ill and you can't go to work? ▶ section 191
> 3 tell Amy you can't help her and go to work at Pizza Palace? ▶ section 192

190 Section 190

'That's good news,' says Ruth. 'See you later.'

Next, you phone Amy. 'What?' she shouts. 'You're not coming? I don't believe* it. Thanks for nothing!' She hangs up the phone. Now you really have a headache*. You take a paracetamol and you go to work. Ruth's waiting for you.

▶ section 200

191 Section 191

You phone Ruth, your boss at Pizza Palace. 'Hello, it's me,' you say. 'I'm sorry, I can't come to work today. I'm ill.'
'Really?' Ruth says. 'What's wrong?'

> **What do you say?**
> 1 'I have flu. I feel terrible.' ▶ section 194
> 2 'I have a headache.' ▶ section 195

192 Section 192

'I'm sorry,' you say. 'I can't help you. I'm working at Pizza Palace.'

'Pizza Palace!' says Amy. She sounds angry. 'Your job at Pizza Palace isn't important. It's not a career! Come to the TV station and help me. Please?'

Chapter 12

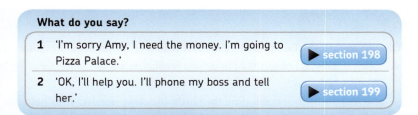

Section 193

When you arrive at the TV studio, there are lots of people and there's a lot of noise. Amy sees you. 'Thank you for coming! I'm so pleased!' she says.

'No problem,' you reply.

'The show begins in five minutes. You can sit anywhere.'

You can sit at the front next to a group of young people. Or there's another seat at the back, between an old couple and a businessman. He's wearing a smart* suit* with a cool* tie.

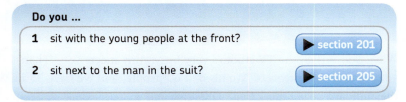

Chapter 12

Section 194

'Oh, no!' says Ruth. 'Don't come to work. If you have flu*, maybe everyone will catch it. Stay at home, OK? I hope you feel better soon!'

'Thanks,' you say.

You feel bad about not telling the truth, but Amy needed your help. You can also meet important business contacts at the show.

▶ section 196

Section 195

'A headache?' says Ruth. 'I have a headache every day! Take a paracetamol and come to work! I'll see you here this afternoon!'

What do you say?

1. 'No, I'm sorry but it's a very bad headache. I can't work today.' ▶ section 197
2. 'OK, you're right. I'll come to work.' ▶ section 190

Section 196

When you arrive, the TV studio's very busy. Amy meets you. 'Thank you for coming!' she says. 'We needed 60 people, and we have 35 in the audience now. I think that's OK!'

'I lied* to my boss, Amy,' you say. 'I told her I was ill.'

'Oh, no! Well, thank you. Don't sit at the front, or your boss will see

Chapter 12

you on TV. Sit at the back. Do you see the man in the business suit?'

'Yes,' you say.

'He's a businessman and they'll interview him on the show. At first, he'll be in the audience. Then he'll come down here for his interview. Sit next to him because he works for a really good company,' says Amy. 'Maybe he can give you a job!'

'Good idea,' you say. 'Thanks, Amy.'

'Sorry, now it's time for me to work.'

 section 205

Section 197

'I see,' says Ruth. 'Well, we'll see you when you feel better. Goodbye!'

She hangs up. She wasn't happy. You're annoyed. Ruth doesn't care about you. Then you remember that you lied about the illness. So she was right to be angry!

You really want to leave Pizza Palace. But how is it possible? Perhaps there'll be an answer at the TV station.

 section 196

Section 198

'I'm so angry!' says Amy. 'Thanks for nothing!' She hangs up. You feel bad.

You go to work. There are lots of customers. There is a TV in Pizza Palace and you can watch Amy's show. The guests are businesspeople. You missed a great opportunity to talk to people about jobs.

Ruth arrives late and she sees you watching TV.

 section 200

Section 199

You phone Ruth, your boss at Pizza Palace, and you explain the situation. 'You can't come to work because you want to go on TV?' Ruth asks.

'Yes,' you say. 'It'll be my first time on TV and I really want to go. They only told me this morning.'

'Well, OK,' says Ruth. 'Next Sunday we have six big

95

Chapter 12

groups of people at Pizza Palace. There'll be 200 people here! If you work all day that Sunday, you can go to the TV show today.'

'OK!' you say. 'Thanks!'

Now you can go to the TV studio.

▶ section 193

200 Section 200

She asks to speak to you alone. She has a piece of paper in her hand. You're worried.

'I got an email from head office*,' Ruth says. 'They're giving you a promotion*. Next month, you'll start as a manager in a new Pizza Palace restaurant! Congratulations!'

It's good news, but you don't feel happy. You don't want to be a manager at Pizza Palace. 'Thanks, Ruth,' you say, 'but please say 'no' to head office. Pizza Palace isn't my dream career.'

Go back to the start of the chapter and try again. ◀ section 189

201 Section 201

The group of young people are very friendly. They're also looking for jobs. 'It's so difficult! I applied for 30 jobs last month. I didn't get one interview!' says one woman.

'I saw an advert* on the internet,' says another man. 'I applied for it online. I got an automatic reply in one minute. It was 'no, thank you'!'

'I have a degree*,' says another man. 'But companies want more than a degree – they want a master's*!'

You tell them about your experience. Then the show starts and you watch it together. The show is fun and you are happy that Amy has an interesting job. At the end, Amy's very busy with the guests. You can't say 'goodbye', so you go home.

You didn't make any job contacts but you learned that a lot of other people have similar problems to you.

▶ section 208

Chapter 12

Section 202

You sit next to the man. You see he has a name badge 'Tom Dilger'.

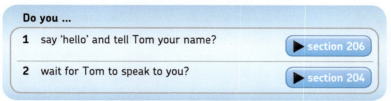

Section 203

⭐ You win 1 bonus point. Mark the scorecard on page 115.
'What are you doing at the moment?' he asks.

'I'm working at Pizza Palace but it's temporary*. I'm looking for a career,' you say.

'Really? My company's looking for some new employees*. We put the job advert* online yesterday. Give you me your business card or your phone number.'

You don't have a business card but you give Tom your telephone number. You want to talk more but the show is starting. Tom is a guest. They speak to him on the show. After the show, everyone wants to talk to Tom, so you can't talk to him again.

Amy's working hard so you go home. Maybe ZQ Central is your big opportunity?

▶ section 208

Section 204

The man looks nervous. You wait for five minutes but he doesn't speak to you. Suddenly, the show starts. Tom's a guest. They interview him on the show.

After the show, everyone wants to speak to Tom so you can't meet him again.

Amy's working hard so you go home. You think about the day. You helped Amy, but going to the TV studio didn't help your job search. You must return to Pizza Palace.

▶ section 208

Chapter 12

205 | Section 205

You smile at the man. His face looks familiar.

Did you meet him at the careers fair in chapter 6?

1 If you met him at the careers fair ▶ section 207

2 If you didn't meet him at the careers fair ▶ section 202

206 | Section 206

Tom Dilger says, 'Hi, I'm the Managing Director of ZQ Central.'

It's a famous company. He's very pleased to speak to you because he doesn't know the other people in the TV studio. He's a guest on the TV show. He's very friendly. 'Here's my card,' he says. Tom gives you his business card. 'My extension is 215.'

Good decision! Write down Tom's extension in the Contacts section on page 115.

▶ section 203

207 | Section 207

It's Tom Dilger. You say 'hello'. At first, Tom doesn't remember you. Then you tell him the story about the thief and the umbrella. He laughs when you tell him the story.

'I remember!' he says. 'You gave me your CV*! I think it's in my office somewhere.'

Tom Dilger's very pleased to speak to you because he doesn't know the other people in the TV studio.

▶ section 203

Chapter 13

Section 208

It's Sunday lunchtime and Pizza Palace is really busy. There are lots of staff* working today and lots of customers and children in the restaurant. It's raining, so people come inside with wet umbrellas, wet coats and wet shoes.

Two small boys are playing in front of the kitchen door. The door opens suddenly and a waiter walks into the restaurant quickly. He's carrying lots of drinks and two pizzas. The door hits the boys and they scream. The waiter falls over and the drinks fall on the boys. They start to cry. A pizza lands on a customer's head, like a big hat.

You're helping to clean the boys when your phone starts ringing. Then it stops. You take the boys to their parents' table. After a few minutes, Pizza Palace is back to normal.

You recognise an umbrella by the door. You pick it up and look at it. It's definitely your umbrella from the careers fair*. Did a Pizza Palace customer take your umbrella at the careers fair? You leave it by the door and decide to watch it.

Your phone rings again. It's Ruth's day off, so this time you look at your phone. 'Private number.'

Chapter 13

> **Do you ...**
>
> 1 answer the phone? Maybe it's an employer. ▶ section 221
>
> 2 decide not to answer the phone? You're at work and it's really busy. ▶ section 216

209 Section 209

You're outside. It's raining. You move ten metres down the street and stand in a shop door. 'Mr Dilger?' you say.

'Hi, yes, I'm still here! That's much better. It was so noisy in there! Where were you?'

'At work. At Pizza Palace.'

'Ah, I see. Well, this won't take long. Are you still looking for a new career?'

'Yes, I am!' you say.

'Good. It's about a job at ZQ Central. It's a junior position and the pay won't be great at first, but there are really good future career opportunities.'

'That's amazing,' you say. Suddenly there's a 'BEEP' in your ear. You look at the screen. Pizza Palace is calling. You decide to ignore* it.

Tom Dilger asks you a few basic questions about yourself. Luckily, you prepared this information when you had the Cyclox Industries interview. The conversation is going really well. There's another 'BEEP' in your ear.

> **Do you ...**
>
> 1 put Tom on 'hold' for a moment and take the call? Maybe it's another emergency, like a fire. ▶ section 210
>
> 2 ignore it? Tom Dilger is more important. ▶ section 214

210 Section 210

'Oh Tom, I'm really sorry,' you say. 'I have another call. Please wait a moment.'

100

Chapter 13

'OK,' says Tom, but he doesn't sound happy. 'My number is 01632 960 0215. Call me in about 30 minutes.'

You answer the other call on your phone. 'Hello?' You say.

It's a recorded voice. 'This is Telephone International. We have a great offer for a new mobile phone. If you change your contract to our company, you'll only pay...'

Oh, no! It's an automatic sales call! You hang up. When you call Tom, you can't speak to him. You speak to his PA. 'Ah, yes, Tom told me about you,' says the PA. 'Come for an interview at our offices at 8.30 a.m. on Tuesday next week. Is that all right?' He gives you the address. Everything's OK! You have an interview at ZQ Central Ltd!

 section 222

Section 211

'Tom Dilger?' you say. 'Of course I remember you! It's very nice to hear from you.'

'Pardon?'

'It's very nice to hear from you.'

'What was that?'

'I said ...' You suddenly stop speaking because a waiter drops a plate next to you. The noise is terrible.

'Sorry, it's very noisy,' says Tom. 'I can't hear anything! Can you go somewhere quiet so we can talk?' The only quiet place is in the street. You'll get cold and wet in the street.

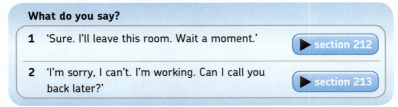

What do you say?

1 'Sure. I'll leave this room. Wait a moment.' ▶ section 212

2 'I'm sorry, I can't. I'm working. Can I call you back later?' ▶ section 213

Section 212

You look up. Darren, the chef, is watching you. You press 'mute' on your phone, so Tom can't hear you.

101

Chapter 13

'I'm really sorry,' you say to Darren. 'This is an important call. Can I go outside for five minutes? I'll work extra at the end of my shift*.'

'That's fine. Take an umbrella! It's raining.'

You remember your umbrella. It's not by the door. Someone took your umbrella again!

 section 209

213 Section 213

'No,' says Tom Dilger. 'This is the only time I can speak this week. I have to go now. Goodbye.' Tom Dilger doesn't call you back and he doesn't return your calls.

Bad luck! Your job search ends here.

Go back to the start of the chapter and try again. ◀ section 208

214 Section 214

⭐ You win 1 bonus point. Mark the scorecard on page 115.

'What's that beeping noise?' asks Tom.

'Nothing,' you say. 'It's just my phone. They're calling me from work.'

'Poor you,' says Tom. 'That happens to me all the time here at ZQ Central.' You both laugh. You and Tom have a good relationship. 'OK. Right,' says Tom. 'I think that's everything for the moment. Can you come for an interview next week?'

Suddenly, a person walks past you in the street. You can't see the person's face, but he has your umbrella!

Do you ...
1 say, 'One moment!' to Tom, and run after the person with your umbrella? ▶ section 218
2 ignore it? Tom's making you an important offer. ▶ section 219

Chapter 13

Section 215

215

It was a good decision to answer the phone. Ruth isn't here and you can't miss a job opportunity. 'Hello?' you say. 'Hello?' You can hear a voice, but you can't hear what it's saying. You turn up the volume. 'Hello?'

'Hi. This is Tom Dilger.'
'Sorry, who?'
'Tom Dilger. From ZQ Central. We met before, do you remember?'
It's your lucky day – the caller is an employer.

▶ section 211

Section 216

216

The number was 'private', so your phone didn't save the caller's number. You don't know who it was, so you can't call them back. You don't get any other job offers for a long time.

Bad luck! Your job search ends here.

Go back to the start of the chapter and try again. ◀ section 208

Section 217

217

The phone call isn't from an employer. It's Simon again. He always phones you at work. 'Hi Simon,' you say. 'I'm sorry, I'm at work. I can't talk at the moment.'
'Oh, sorry. I just wanted to tell you, I've got a great new job.'
'Really? That's … great.'
'Yes, it is. I'm going out to celebrate. Can you come?'
'No, I can't. I have to work my shift here.'
'Bad luck,' he says and hangs up the phone.

103

Chapter 13

You're very disappointed*. Mark, Amy and now Simon have all got good jobs and you're still working at Pizza Palace. 'What did I do wrong?' you ask yourself.

To complete your job search, you need to talk to Tom Dilger.

You have two options

1. Go back to the beginning of chapter 6 and meet Tom at the careers fair.   section 77

2. Go back to the beginning of chapter 12 and meet Tom at the TV studio.   section 189

218 Section 218

You run after the person with your umbrella. 'Stop!' you shout. 'That's my umbrella!' The person turns around. It's Simon. 'Simon! Why have you got my umbrella?' you ask. You're *very* surprised.

▶ section 220

219 Section 219

It was a good decision to ignore* the umbrella. This is an important call. 'Sorry?' you say.

'Can you come for an interview next week?'

'Yes, please, Mr Dilger. Thank you! I'd be delighted.'

'Call me Tom.'

'Thank you, Tom. That sounds great.'

'Great. Come to our offices at 8.30 on Tuesday next week.'

'OK, I'll see you at 8.30 on Tuesday morning. Thanks and goodbye.'

You're very excited. This is a great opportunity. After work, you do some research* on ZQ Central. You also look at your notes about yourself. You feel ready for anything now.

 section 222

Chapter 13

Section 220

'Hi! You're getting wet!' Simon says. 'Stand under my umbrella.'

'But this isn't your umbrella,' you say. 'It's mine! I lost it at a careers fair.'

'I don't know what you mean. This is Amy's umbrella.'

'Amy's umbrella?'

'Yes,' says Simon. 'Amy gave it to me a few weeks ago. Why …?'

'It doesn't matter,' you say, and you return to your phone conversation with Tom. 'Hello Tom, sorry about that.' There's no reply. 'Hello, Tom?' He didn't wait for you. He hung up. It wasn't a good idea to run after the umbrella.

You call ZQ Central five times but Tom doesn't call you back. You don't get any other job offers for a long time.

Bad luck! Your job search ends here.

Go back to the start of the chapter and try again.

Section 221

Look at the Contacts section on page 115.

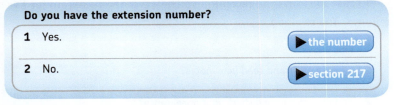

105

Chapter 14

222 Section 222

You arrive on time at the ZQ Central offices. It's early morning and the company's employees are arriving for work. They're laughing and chatting. It looks like a friendly place to work. When you arrive, you meet the receptionist. 'I'm sorry, Tom's in a meeting. He'll be ten minutes late,' says the receptionist. 'Please wait here.' You sit down in reception and notice that one wall is a mirror. You can see your reflection.

'Excuse me,' says the receptionist. He leaves the reception for five minutes. You're alone.

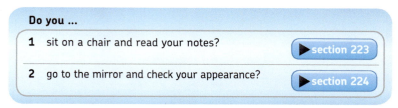

223 Section 223

You read your notes and a news article about the company. You remember lots of facts to use in your interview. After five minutes, the receptionist returns. He takes you into the next room to meet Tom Dilger. Tom isn't alone. There's also an assistant in the room. During the interview, the assistant never speaks.

Chapter 14

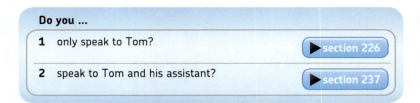

Section 224

You look in the mirror. You check your hair and your teeth. You check your clothes. Then the receptionist returns. He laughs for a moment. 'You can go into your interview now,' he says. He opens the door next to the mirror and you go into a room. There are two people in the room – Tom and another woman.

Suddenly, you see that the wall was only a mirror in the reception. In this room, the same wall is glass! They watched you check your teeth, hair and clothes. You feel very embarrassed*. 'Come in,' says Tom. 'It's nice to meet you again. Sit down. This is my assistant, Carmen.'

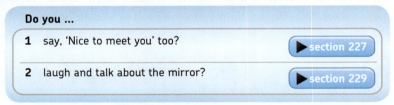

Section 225

'This is a great offer,' says Tom. 'The salary* will get much better after a year. This is a career with a future. If you can't see that, you're the wrong person for my company.'

'No, I'm sorry. I'm happy with the money,' you reply.

'Well, if we want to work with you, we'll call you,' says Tom. 'Goodbye and thank you for coming.'

You go home and wait for Tom Dilger's call. He never calls you.
Bad luck! Your job search ends here.

Go back to the start of the chapter and try again. ◀ section 222

Chapter 14

Section 226

Tom asks you some questions and you give good answers. You feel confident. Then Tom asks you a difficult question. 'Imagine you're in a dangerous situation at work,' he says. 'For example, imagine there's a fire. Everyone's panicking. What do you do?'

You think for a moment. Then you remember the fire at Pizza Palace.

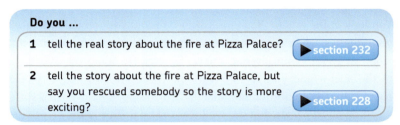

Do you …

1. tell the real story about the fire at Pizza Palace? ▶ section 232
2. tell the story about the fire at Pizza Palace, but say you rescued somebody so the story is more exciting? ▶ section 228

Section 227

'Let's start the interview,' says Tom. His assistant doesn't speak but she writes notes. 'Why do you think you are a good candidate* for the job?'

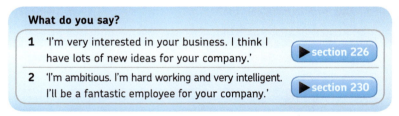

What do you say?

1. 'I'm very interested in your business. I think I have lots of new ideas for your company.' ▶ section 226
2. 'I'm ambitious. I'm hard working and very intelligent. I'll be a fantastic employee for your company.' ▶ section 230

Section 228

Tom is very surprised that you rescued somebody. He asks you lots of questions about it. Because you didn't tell him the truth, you make mistakes when you answer. Tom and his assistant don't think your story is true.

Tom asks you some more questions and then he ends the interview. 'Thank you very much for coming today,' he says. 'If you're successful, we'll call you.' You go home and wait for Tom's call. The phone never rings.

Chapter 14

Bad luck! Your job search ends here.

Go back to the start of the chapter and try again. section 222

Section 229

229

'I feel really stupid!' you say. 'You saw me in the mirror. I didn't know! Ha, ha, ha!'

Tom and his assistant don't laugh. 'Yes, people often make that mistake,' says Tom. You feel more embarrassed. You start to panic. You don't answer Tom's questions well. At the end of the interview, he doesn't offer you the job.

Bad luck! Your job search ends here.

Go back to the start of the chapter and try again. section 222

Section 230

230

'Really?' Tom says. He doesn't sound very interested in your answer.

What do you say?

1 'One more thing, I really want to learn more about your business.' ▶ section 231
2 'One more thing, can I earn a lot of money in this industry?' ▶ section 234

Section 231

231

'Excellent,' says Tom. He asks you some more questions. They are the same questions from your interviews with Carol Tree and at Cyclox Industries. You give very good answers to them. Tom and his assistant look very pleased. 'One more thing,' says Tom. 'The salary. Now, we don't pay a lot in the beginning, but you'll get a lot of training*. Later, the salary will increase.' He tells you the starting salary. The money is 10% lower than your salary at Pizza Palace.

'So, do you want to work here?' asks Tom.

109

Chapter 14

232 Section 232

⭐ You win 1 bonus point. Mark the scorecard on page 115.

'That's amazing,' says Tom, when you finish your story. 'Personally, I think it was a great idea to work at Pizza Palace. Any job is good experience. You learn about working in teams.'

Good decision! Both Tom and his assistant write some notes.

233 Section 233

'Yes, but you work for a fast food restaurant,' says Tom. 'Your salary won't go up in the future.'

234 Section 234

'The right person can earn a good salary,' says Tom. He sounds disappointed. He asks you some more questions but he doesn't seem very interested in your answers.

At the end of the interview, you go home and wait for his phone call. The phone never rings.

Bad luck! Your job search ends here.

Go back to the start of the chapter and try again.

235 Section 235

'This is a great career opportunity,' you say, 'and I'd love to work for ZQ Central.'

Chapter 14

'That's good news,' says Tom.
You want to negotiate the salary.

What do you say?

1. 'Is it possible to increase the salary? At the moment, it's lower than my pay at Pizza Palace.' section 233

2. 'Is it possible to increase the salary? I saw that similar jobs in the industry have a higher salary.' ▶ section 236

Section 236

'That's true,' says Tom, 'our competitors* pay more money. But at ZQ Central, we give you lots of training and we're the best company in the business. People love working for us. Remember that this is only the starting salary.'

What do you say?

1. 'Yes, ZQ Central is a great company, but is it be possible to increase the salary by 5%?' ▶ section 225

2. 'OK then, I'm happy with the salary and I'll accept the job.' ▶ section 238

Section 237

⭐ You win 1 bonus point. Mark the scorecard on page 115.
Good decision! Tom is pleased that you think about other people. His assistant doesn't speak to you, but she smiles.

▶ section 226

Ending

238 Section 238

'I'm so pleased,' says Tom. 'The job is yours.'

'That's great,' you reply. You shake hands.

'Congratulations!' says Tom. 'This is a good company to work for. Everyone's friendly here and we have a great future ahead of us. You were the best candidate* in all my interviews.'

'I'm so pleased,' you say. 'Thank you so much for this job offer!' You're very happy. You have one more question. 'When will I start?' you ask.

'Is next Monday OK with you?' Tom replies.

'Next Monday's perfect,'

'Now, I have a surprise for you,' says Tom.

'What's that?' you ask.

'As you know, ZQ Central work with lots of big companies, and in your first project I want you to work with a very important company – a company that you already know.'

'Really?' you say, 'Which company?'

'We want you to work on the project for Pizza Palace. Sorry, there's no escape for you!'

Everyone laughs. You leave the office and phone your friends and family. Everyone is very happy for you. You've got the job of your dreams!

Ending

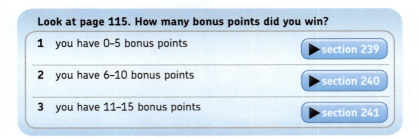

Section 239

Well done! You got the job of your dreams, but you didn't win many bonus points.

You work hard at ZQ Central, but the project for Pizza Palace doesn't go well. The next project you work on isn't a success* either. After one year, Tom Dilger asks to speak to you in his office.

'Sit down,' he says. 'I've got some bad news.'

You sit down and ask, 'What's the problem?'

'We don't think ZQ Central is the right company for you. I'm sorry, but you have to leave.'

You're very sad. You have to look for another job.

Try the maze again and see if you can win more bonus points.

Section 240

Well done! You got the job of your dreams, and you won quite a lot of bonus points.

You work hard at ZQ Central and the project for Pizza Palace is a big success*. The next project you work on goes well, too. After one year Tom Dilger asks to speak to all the employees* at ZQ Central.

'Hello everybody,' he says. 'I've got some fantastic news. ZQ Central is a very successful company and we want to grow. Next year, we'll open an office in New York and we want one of you to be the manager in the new office. If you're interested, please apply* to Carmen, my assistant.'

You apply for the job. One month later, Tom asks to speak to you

Ending

in his office.

'Sit down,' he says. 'It's about the New York manager job.'

You sit down and ask, 'Have you got any news?'

'I'm sorry, but we can't give you the job,' he says. 'You're a very good candidate, and your work is excellent, but we chose somebody else.'

'OK,' you say, 'I understand.'

You're a little disappointed*, but you have a great job that you enjoy a lot.

Try the maze again and see if you can win more bonus points.

241 Section 241

Well done! You got the job of your dreams, and you won lots of bonus points.

You work hard at ZQ Central and the project for Pizza Palace is a big success*. The next project you work on goes well, too. After one year Tom Dilger asks to speak to all the employees* at ZQ Central.

'Hello everybody,' he says. 'I've got some fantastic news. ZQ Central is a very successful company and we want to grow. Next year, we'll open an office in New York and we want one of you to be the manager in the new office. If you're interested, please apply* to Carmen, my assistant.'

You apply for the job. One month later, Tom asks to speak to you in his office.

'Sit down,' he says. 'It's about the New York manager job.'

You sit down and ask, 'Have you got any news?'

'Yes, I have and it's good news. You did a fantastic job with the Pizza Palace project and your work is excellent. We think you're the best person to manage the New York office.'

'Wow! That's fantastic. I don't know what to say.'

'Congratulations!' Tom smiles and shakes your hand.

You're very excited. You're going on a new adventure to New York.

The end

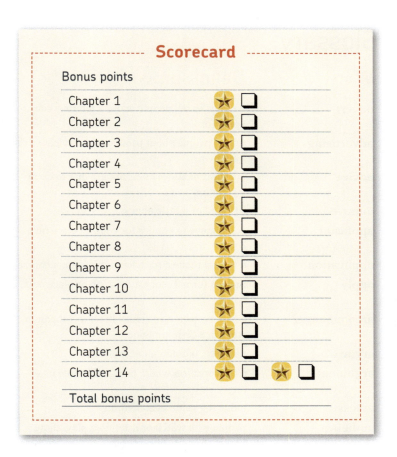

Glossary

Word	Definition
advert	a notice to tell people about a job they can apply for
advertising	telling people about products or services so they buy them
advice	opinions or suggestions about what to do in a situation
annoyed	irritated or a little angry
applicant	someone who applies for a job or place on a course
application	a formal request for a job or place on a course
apply	make a formal request for a job or place on a course
area manager	someone who is responsible for a company's work in a certain region
argue	disagree, often in an angry way
argument	a conversation where people disagree in an angry way
assess	judge the value of something
audience	people who watch or listen to a play, show, programme or concert
believe	think that something or someone is true or right
boss	someone who is in charge of someone at work and tells them what to do
bossy	likes to tell other people what to do
candidate	someone who has applied for a job
career	a series of jobs that someone has in their life
careers fair	an event where people who want a job can meet employers
chat	talk in an informal, friendly way
chat show	a television programme where famous people answer questions informally

Glossary

clever	able to learn or understand things quickly
competitor	another company in the same sector
complain	say that something is wrong or you are not satisfied
colleague	someone you work with
confident	having a strong belief in yourself and your abilities
contract	an official agreement about the conditions of a job
cool	fashionable, attractive and popular
CV	a written description of your education and jobs you have done
degree	the award a university gives you when you complete a course
disappointed	unhappy because something didn't happen or wasn't successful
e-commerce	business that is carried out on the internet
editor	someone who is in charge of a newspaper and decides what to publish
editorial assistant	someone who helps editors publish a newspaper, magazine or books
elevator	a machine used to move up and down to other levels in a building
embarrassed	feeling shy or uncomfortable because of something you did
employee	someone who works for a company
employer	a company that pays people to do work for them
expert	someone who has a lot of skill or knowledge about something
fame	being known or recognised by many people
fee	the amount of money a service costs
fire extinguisher	a device used to stop small fires
flu	a common illness that causes headaches and fever

Glossary

font	the style or size of letters used in printing
formal	suitable for important events and official ceremonies
free	not busy or having anything planned
full-time	for a complete working week
head office	the main office where managers make important decisions
headache	a continuous pain in your head
hobby	an activity which you do for pleasure or to relax
Human Resources (HR)	the department of a company which deals with the employees
ignore	to notice something, but not give attention to it
interview	a formal meeting where an employer discovers if someone is suitable for a job
jobseeker	someone who is trying to find a job
journalist	someone who writes about news stories for the media
knowledge	information gained through education or experience
leadership	the ability of someone to lead
lie	to deliberately not tell the truth or deceive somebody
master's	a higher level degree that you study after a first degree
minimum wage	the lowest amount of money that an employer can legally pay an employee
order	a request for a meal
Personal Assistant (PA)	someone who organises and helps a more senior person
pan	a deep pot used for cooking
part-time	working for only part of the day or week
permanent	lasting for a long time or forever
profile	a description of someone or list of facts about them

Glossary

promotion	getting a more important job than you had before
queue	a line of people who are waiting
recruitment agent	a person who provides organisations with employees
reference	a written report of someone's character, skills and achievements
refuse	to say 'no' to something you have been offered
register	to record your name on a list
reply	an answer to an email someone has sent to you
research	investigate a certain subject
salary	the amount of money paid to an employee every year
scared	frightened or afraid
selection process	a series of actions that help to choose the best option
shift	the hours of the day when you have to work
shy	timid, nervous, easily frightened
smart	clean, neat and formal clothing
staff	a group of employees that work at an organisation
stand	a place which provides information
success	the achievement of a desired aim
successful	something that has achieved the desired aim
suit	a set of clothes, usually a jacket and trousers
task	a piece of work
teamwork skills	ability to work successfully with a group of people
temporary	not permanent, effective for a short period of time
thief	a person who steals
training	the combination of practice and learning
warning	saying the bad consequences of an action
waste	to use something unproductively

58 St Aldates
Oxford
OX1 1ST
United Kingdom

© 2014, Santillana Educación, S.L. / Richmond

Publisher: Ruth Goodman
Editor(s): David Cole-Powney, Hannah Champney
Digital Publisher: Luke Baxter
Senior Digital Editor: Belen Fernandez
Software Developers: Avallain
Digital Management: Haremi
Design Manager: Lorna Heaslip
Logo Design: Russell Hrachovec at compoundEye
Design & Layout: Lorna Heaslip
Picture Editor: Magdalena Mayo

ISBN: 978-84-668-1743-1

First edition: 2014

Printed in Brazil
DL: M-1296-2014

No unauthorised copying
All rights reserved. No part of this book may be reproduced, stored in a retrieval system or transmitted in any form by any means, electronic, mechanical, photocopying, recording or otherwise, without the prior permission in writing of the Publisher.

Photographs:
iStockphoto; ARCHIVO SANTILLANA

Illustrations:
Aleix Pons Oliver

Audio:
Motivation Sound Studios, www.motivationsound.co.uk; Sound Jay, www.soundjay.com

Every effort has been made to trace the holders of copyright before publication. The Publisher will be pleased to rectify any errors or omissions at the earliest opportunity.

Impressão: Forma Certa Gráfica Digital
Lote: 782117
Cód.: 290517431